Belinda Grant has a com
and personal growth whic
when she first consulted a
studied and worked with
porating them into her na
and works in London whe
occasional radio broadcast

OPTIMA

THE DETOX DIET BOOK

BELINDA GRANT

An OPTIMA book

© Belinda Grant 1991

First published in 1991 by
Macdonald Optima, a division of
Macdonald & Co. (Publishers) Ltd

A member of Maxwell Macmillan Pergamon Publishing Corporation

All Rights Reserved

No part of this publication may be reproduced,
stored in a retrieval system, or transmitted,
in any form or by any means, without the prior
permission in writing of the publisher, nor be
otherwise circulated in any form of binding or
cover other than that in which it is published
and without a similar condition including this
condition being imposed on the subsequent
purchaser.

British Library Cataloguing in Publication Data
Grant, Belinda
  The detox diet book.
  1. Man. Diet
  I. Title
  613.7

ISBN 0-356-19610-0

Macdonald & Co. (Publishers) Ltd
Orbit House
1 New Fetter Lane
London EC4A 1AR

Typeset in Century Schoolbook by Leaper & Gard Ltd, Bristol

Printed and bound in Great Britain by Cox & Wyman Ltd, Reading

For Nora and Henry Viagas

CONTENTS

Acknowledgements	ix
1. Introduction	1
2. Why Detoxify?	4
3. The History of It All	10
4. 'Yes' Foods	18
5. 'No' Foods	26
6. Your Detox Plan	30
7. Stage I	35
8. Stage II	41
9. Stage III	59
10. Not Just Foods	66
11. Most Common Questions	72
12. Exercise	79
13. Optional Extras	84
14. Putting It Into Practice	91
15. Clear Your Mind	97
16. A Word for Women	105
Finding A Practitioner	109
Further Reading	110
Index	111

ACKNOWLEDGEMENTS

With thanks to Reina James and Mike Reinstein for their constant encouragement, support and practical advice. Betty Balcombe acted as consultant on historical details and her critical appraisal and clarity were invaluable. Terry Boyes provided many recipes, and Sandra Boyes made delivery possible with her computer skills and good humour.

1.
INTRODUCTION

We normally associate detox programmes with alcohol or drug withdrawal, issues which have become headline news in recent years as Hollywood legends and rock stars reveal their life stories. But even those of us who don't take recreational drugs, smoke or drink heavily can still derive great benefit from cleansing our systems of impurities and toxins.

The chemicals and pollutants present in our food, drinking water and the air we breathe make for a complicated cocktail of substances, all compounding the stress of modern-day living. Add to that time constraints and other external stresses, with a dash of genetic material, and bingo! — you have a highly volatile mixture.

This detox programme was devised by developing the simplest, most straightforward naturopathic principle — that your body has its own innate vitality and its own drive for optimum health. If you stop interfering with that basic life force, it will do its best job.

In practice this means no more confusing your body with chemical additives, no more reliance on your adrenal system for energy instead of getting it from well-digested food and no more expecting your body to function without help.

Many of the low-grade illnesses so common today are due to an overload reaction. This occurs when the body is no longer able to handle stress. Symptoms such as endless colds, allergies, that 'need-a-tonic' feeling and constantly cold hands and feet are often the first signs of a failing immune system and a sluggish metabolism.

In 1987, I began working on a stress management programme with a team of health professionals from different disciplines. We incorporated relaxation techniques, recognition skills, massage, counselling and a dietary detox plan into a life-management course. The most profound and long-lasting benefits were gained by those following the detox diet.

The principles of naturopathy — that is, encouraging the body to heal itself — easily lend themselves to everyday health care. Even in the most urban or artificial situation, our bodies work in the same way that they have done for centuries. They will respond to gentle encouragement and stimulation, and are always moving towards optimum health and vitality if given a chance.

The belief that 'only nature heals' has been proven countless times. For me, it explains everything from 'spontaneous remissions' in life-threatening illness, to the fact that when I have a fever, I have no appetite for food and no energy to do anything, other than fight off whatever is causing it.

Our bodies' needs are pure and simple, but they can become warped and easily misinterpreted. For example, we are educated to think of coffee as an instant energy booster. It is vaunted as the way to start your day, the perfect pick-me-up if you hit an energy slump, and also an aid to digestion (!). Pretty soon, your brain learns that if your energy is low, coffee is the answer. This learned habit becomes a physical dependency too.

That high-energy feeling is very seductive, and we begin to think that coffee might be a staple, necessary part of our daily diet. The same holds true for sugar, alcohol and many other substances that all cloud the true picture of our bodies' needs. It is easy, however, to clear that picture and re-establish effective communication between your body and your responses to it. Every day I see people strengthen these connections as they find a pocket of simplicity in their busy lives.

A huge variety of people have followed this programme throughout the years I have been in practice. It is effective for young and old alike, and the only people who should not undertake it without supervision are those under 18 years of age, and anyone with a serious illness. Pregnant women should not do it at all, but the programme is a perfect preparation for both partners seeking to start a family.

Terry Boyes, a caterer by profession, first undertook this detox programme in 1986. She has become a devout believer in following the dictates of her own body, and after witnessing the wonderful benefits to her health, returns yearly to a month's detoxification. Many of the recipes in this book have been created by her.

A large number of the people I see in my practice suffer with a similar range of symptoms. They have a conspicuous lack of vital energy overlying any deep-seated or individual problem. All respond to a variation of the detox plan, and find relief from symptoms as wide-ranging as headaches and piles. Following a detox diet is also the only effective way of eliminating cellulite. And, of course, all return to a sustainable energy level which is the key to all long term health care.

2. WHY DETOXIFY?

This is a book for healthy people who are under siege. People who can't say there is anything *really* wrong with them, but can never get their feet warm in winter, or don't really have enough energy; people who often get headaches, or don't sleep well; women with period problems. People suffering from indigestion, constipation, suppressed libido; all those very real difficulties that nevertheless do not feel like any serious illness. All of us, in fact, suffering from the stressful pace and environmental pressures of twentieth-century living.

This programme will cleanse and revitalise your body systems, boost your immune function and stabilise your energy needs. That means an end to allergies, weight fluctuations and recurring ailments.

Our bodies are marvellously resourceful, and can manage for long periods with adequate or sub-adequate nutrition, and deal with high levels of stress. Sooner or later, however, something gives. Many of the degenerative diseases of middle and older age that we take for granted can be directly attributed to our own lifestyles.

Our bodies know the secrets of good health — locked in to our distant memory is an eating plan linked to the seasons. By harnessing this natural phenomenon (and adding a little extra effort) we can give ourselves the rejuvenating fillip we could all benefit from.

This dynamic, natural programme de-stresses your whole body, restoring vitality and health. Based on the simple principle of getting rid of stresses wherever possible, the benefits of the detox diet will give you a fitter body, a clearer mind and higher spirits.

We are constantly striving for balance. At a cellular level this means our complicated biochemical harmony is continually being monitored and adapted. This method of adaptation has been refined through centuries of change. Today, we are faced with a greater number of external changes, and change at a much faster pace, than our internal mechanisms have ever encountered. Alongside the pressures of a hectic lifestyle then, we experience tremendous stresses in our own bodies.

For one month, you will be following a system of natural medicine that is safe and effective. Actively cleansing your body of a lifetime's build up of impurities and obstacles to good health will yield remarkable benefits.

THE EFFECTS OF STRESS

In our everyday lives, so many of us feel less than a hundred per cent healthy. Even those without specific health problems experience times when they feel sluggish and do not have the energy they need. Resorting to sugar, endless cups of coffee and other stimulants to keep us mentally on-the-ball is not the answer. How, though, should we cope with our ever-increasing need for more time, and the stress we feel as a result?

Stress can be divided into two main categories — external and internal. External stresses like time constraints, pressure of work and financial worries generate an internal response. This adds to any physical problems or deficiencies we may already have to create inner stress.

Our reaction to most difficulties is to rise and meet them or to flee from them — our 'fight or flight' response. What happens is that our adrenal glands produce large amounts of adrenalin in response to any stressful stimulus. This provides the energy needed to either run like the wind or stand and fight.

Our bodies react in this way to many of the crises we face. All are treated as life-threatening, although most do not warrant this level of response. Of course, we are not literally fighting for our lives, or running to save our skins, so this tremendous energy is not used. Nevertheless, all our muscles are on standby; we are more mentally alert and our hearts are beating faster. All our available energy is switched away from digesting and assimilating nutrients and all the other internal jobs that, in its crisis-dealing mode, the body deems non-vital.

If you spend a day in this state, it means that while you are always ready to defend your life, you will have absorbed little nourishment from your food and you will have done none of the essential maintenance and repair work needed for continued good health. In fact, many of us spend most of our lives in this state. Little wonder, then, that we begin to suffer malabsorption problems, an inability to relax, constant nervous irritation and, eventually, the possibility of chronic disease.

A large number of degenerative diseases are directly related to over-use and overload: over-use of compounds that the body is not naturally equipped to deal with; overload on the body's eliminative routes and organs.

When our systems are overloaded, there have to be cutbacks — we reject the things that require the most energy to process — so some energy-packed foods and many that are chemically complex begin to be rejected and treated as allergens. Our bodies switch erratically from concentrating on food assimilation to ignoring digestive function in favour of other pressing needs. This can cause huge weight fluctuations. Poor bowel health occurs with the continuous change in the quality and quantity of material passing through it, leading to bouts of constipation and diarrhoea, and possibly to piles and even greater difficulties. Gallstones and liver congestion can occur as fat metabolism becomes more difficult, and indigestion, acid dyspepsia and ulcers can make eating anything at all quite uncomfortable.

Although much can be done to reduce specific external stresses, we must also give our bodies the time and energy they need to maintain good health. If we add problem

WHY DETOXIFY?

foods (those which are difficult to digest, like cow's milk) and poisons (things the body needs to expel immediately, like pesticides) to our daily diet, we overload our digestive systems and create yet another huge need for energy.

This detox programme will provide all the immediate energy needed to carry on with everyday life, while ensuring that there are ample resources available for all the background healing work that must be done. No more crisis management, in fact, but good all-round housekeeping.

Lots of people follow weight reduction diets, or health improvement diets. These can induce their own stresses — having to watch everything you eat or count calories for the rest of your life is a terrible sentence. It can result in feelings of depression, obsessive behaviour, or at the very least, leave you feeling continually deprived. Your metabolism slows down, too, if the amount you eat is restricted, so you end up with less energy, and minimal weight loss.

The benefits of this one-month programme are legion. Not least among them is the fact that because it is so short term, you can be extravagant in the measures you use to regain full health. Thirty days of concerted effort is certainly manageable.

The diet plan lasts for four weeks, and although there are dietary changes involved, the transition to a wider eating plan is made easy by the resultant changes in your food wants and the state of your taste buds. That means your health will benefit for the rest of the year from the work done in this month.

It is as recently as the sixteenth century that minutes began to be used as a record of time, and seconds entered common usage in the seventeenth century. Now we are seeing the introduction of the computer-inspired nanosecond.

Our body systems have taken centuries to evolve to their current level of sophistication. In terms of our overall development, the introduction of foods such as wheat occurred only a second ago. Current processing methods that alter the chemical and physical structure of our foods, and the introduction of preservatives and additives happened but a nano-second ago.

How our bodies will adapt to these changes is a question that may not be answered for many years. It will take lengthy research and wide clinical testing to isolate these substances and record our reaction to them. We are already seeing changes, however, in terms of allergies to these and other common substances, along with alterations in the occurrence of birth defects, changes in the pattern of chronic disease and the spread of viruses.

Our bodies are still responding to the time clock our ancestors knew. Only a hundred years ago, the sun, the moon and the seasons governed crop production and the harvest. For centuries the only methods of food storage were drying and salting. Now we can eat strawberries in the middle of winter and root vegetables in August. This creates an amount of internal confusion — meaning our bodies must work harder to obtain nourishment from each meal. Eating what is *naturally* available, that is, eating with the seasons, makes good sense.

Spring is a time of new shoots and spring vegetables, the salad crop. Light and tender after the heavier winter fare, this crop is very welcome in its freshness, and in its marking of the beginning of the year. In ancient calendars the new year fell at the Spring Equinox on 21st March, about the time of the first real crop.

With the first fresh food after winter's dried and stored fare comes a time for the body to rest from heavy, reconstituted foods. Time to increase exercise, fresh air and sunshine, and speed up the metabolism after the winter rest. Food intake is restricted to a minimal variety but there is an ample abundance. This is the perfect opportunity for the body to begin to slough off some of the toxins accumulated through the winter months of calorie-laden food and deal with the body's response of a more sluggish metabolism.

Harnessing the energy of spring with its impulse for renewal is the central theme of this book. Following our innate body-sense, spring is the ideal time to detoxify.

WHY DETOXIFY?

Although there are dietary plans that will serve in other seasons, this programme is perfectly suited for spring and summer.

Undertaken once a year, this month-long clear out will stimulate immune function, strengthen your basic constitution and gently erode any long-standing health deficiencies. Many bad eating habits will get lost along the way and a greater understanding of how your body works will naturally follow.

It seems our ancestors knew the way forward. This dietary plan originated with them. Combined with our current knowledge of how the body works, and modern standards of hygiene, it means we have available to us a simple and effective formula for life-long good health.

3.
THE HISTORY OF IT ALL

We all know that food gives us energy, can provide us with vitamins and minerals, and can be divided into groups — some supplying protein, some fat, some carbohydrate, and so on. An understanding of these elements is essential for a healthy balanced diet. Broadly speaking, we need protein, vitamins and minerals for body maintenance and repair. Carbohydrates and fat supply us with energy, and fat is needed for the absorption of some vitamins.

Foods have other benefits too. Some people say you take on the energy or essence of the foods you eat. They maintain that if an animal is killed cruelly, for example, then you will absorb some of that anxiety when you eat its flesh. This belief has a basis in fact — when an animal is frightened its system is flooded with adrenalin. Not only does this make the meat less tender, but it could also be argued that you will absorb large amounts of adrenalin with your meal. One of the effects of this powerful substance in your body is the shutting down of the flow of energy to your digestive system.

Some people believe you become what you eat, and assess foods by their esoteric qualities. The personal qualities of resolution and solidity could therefore be enhanced by eating beef, while chicken could help one pay attention to detail. They hold the same to be true for excess, however, and attribute bullish behaviour and pickiness respectively to any overindulgence in these foods. (In the light of the development of bovine spongiform encephalitis (BSE), I don't think beef should be eaten at all unless the source is well known.)

THE HISTORY OF IT ALL

This belief also has some basis in fact. Your body is constantly regenerating. New bone is laid down, new skin is made and every cell has a cycle of renewal. This growth comes from the building blocks you supply to your body in the food that you eat.

Many religions have dietary rules which pay attention to the environment of a particular food or its place in mythology. It is said that the Hindu god Yama once blessed the sesame seed, and throughout the East it is regarded as a symbol of immortality.

The use of foods as medicines is noted in the earliest records of civilisation. In Ancient Egypt, the specific qualities of foods were widely known and found everyday application. There were no custodians of this knowledge — it was free and in use by everyone. Papyrus documents from about 1600 B.C. list in their hieroglyphys 876 remedies using over 500 different substances as cures. One of Egypt's greatest goddesses, Isis, schooled her students in many skills before sending them off to share their knowledge with the other peoples of the world. Among the important messages they carried was the use of everyday foods and herbs as remedies. A look at the shared folk remedies throughout the Mediterranean region and the rest of Europe bears witness to the success of these travels.

Countries as far apart as Greece and England find in their common lore the wisdom of the yarrow flower as a kidney tonic; raspberry leaves as a smooth-muscle relaxant; onions and parsley as blood cleansers. From both Spain and Ireland come the use of cobwebs to stop bleeding and honey as a cure for skin infections. The dandelion is valued in France and Italy for its powerful diuretic action, and the beetroot's claim to fame as a liver tonic is held true in Romania and Portugal.

Around 3000 B.C. the Chinese Emperor Fu Hsi was investigating the science of agriculture and its effects on the body, and today herbs and foods form a powerful part of traditional Chinese medicine. In India around 800 B.C., Brahmanistic records list hundreds of plants and herbs known for their healing properties.

THE HISTORY OF IT ALL

As various organized religious beliefs took hold in different parts of the world, the first real signs of hostility towards this everyday system of healthcare came to light. The idea that illnesses were sent by a god gave birth to the notion that only prayer could cure them. It began to be thought blasphemous to cure physical ills by natural, physical means. Combined with the concept of deferred gratification — the idea that suffering in life may lead to rewards after death — natural healing methods began to be usurped.

By the Middle Ages, although herbal remedies and folk medicines were widely used, Europe was in the grip of frenzied attacks on wise women and witches, leading to many being burned for their sorcery. In many instances, the crime of these women was in recognising and using the 'fruits of the forest, the gifts of the earth' for their healing qualities. Today, we distil the active properties from these 'fruits and gifts' in laboratories, and have sophisticated marketing and retail outlets for them. Taking aspirin from willow trees and heart drugs from foxgloves, our laboratories are today busy analysing the mulberry bush for the possibility of an HIV-virus inhibitor.

We need to re-learn the secrets of our food cupboards, and recognise not only the nutrient value of what we eat, but also the health-enhancing qualities of our everyday food. The success of this detox programme stems in part from the remarkable qualities of the foods themselves.

ORGANIC FOODS

There is quite a difference between organic and non-organic foods. Organically grown foods obtain their vitamins, minerals, and nutrients from a well-kept soil. Non-organic foods try to grow in 'dead' soil, and have to be artificially fed with chemical fertilisers and treated with pesticides, insecticides, fungicides, etc. It makes sense to eat 'live' food, that contains the vitamins and minerals it is supposed to, and can therefore nourish you.

There is a strong argument for eating organic foods while

THE HISTORY OF IT ALL

following the detox programme, even if you choose to eat non-organic foods the rest of the time.

By eating as cleanly and simply as you can throughout the programme, you are detoxifying your system; giving your body a rest and enabling it to catch up on the backlog of body maintenance and repair work. The strength and success of this programme depends on encouraging your body's natural ability to slough off poisons and pollutants. Why give it more while it's trying to do this job?

Because non-organic food is grown in dead or near-dead soil, the vital nutrients the plants need are simply not provided in their natural form. Rather like the difference between sugar and saccharine (although I am certainly *not* promoting sugar as a good or natural food) — they both taste the same, but the chemical differences are tremendous. And your body, after all, relates to the micronutrients in foods by recognising their chemical formulae. It may fool your palate, but it will not fool those sophisticated enzyme systems whose job is to recognise the real thing and ignore, and find a way to deal with, imposters.

In my own practice, I have seen countless occasions when an allergy or sensitivity to a particular food or food group has been remedied once the chemicals and additives have been ousted. Once the real food is eaten in its natural form, the allergy dies down, often completely, leading me to propose that the sensitivity was not to the food at all, but to the chemical additives. Although this is a long way from being scientifically proven, I have witnessed it enough times to be convinced that it is certainly worth trying.

For years I suffered from an allergy to apples that is not uncommon. Whenever I ate just a small amount of that fruit my lips and mouth would become sore and be covered with a red rash that would last for hours. That never happens when I eat organically grown apples.

There are tremendous psychological benefits from knowing that you are doing *everything* possible to make your detox programme a success. And organically grown fruit and vegetables taste *so* much better. Once you have eaten an organically grown cucumber or lettuce, I'm sure

THE HISTORY OF IT ALL

you'll be convinced. These foods might not look so bright and shiny, or all be of uniform size, but that is because they are grown rather than manufactured! Coming directly to the shop, they have not been waxed to make them look better, or gassed or irradiated to lengthen their shelf life.

Supermarkets often claim that we will not buy smaller than usual apples, or pears with a speckled skin. They claim these cosmetic treatments are of vital importance. The problem is, that although you may be holding the most aesthetically pleasing apple or bunch of grapes in the world, its nutritional value is suspect, and all that wax isn't very good for you either.

Farming organically is an expensive business. Initially it may take many years of feeding and tending the soil to bring it up to a quality that will produce good crops. This is especially the case if the land has previously been used for a non-organic crop. This care for the earth and the labour-intensive method of working mean that the profit margin for the farmer is very small. The government is currently looking into ways to make these early years less punishing, and if successful in assigning grants or tax incentives to organic farmers, then we should see the price of organic food drop considerably. Alternatively, if the introduction of heavy fines for chemical dumping and pesticide pollution was adopted, more and more farmers would have to look to organic methods, as farming the chemical way could become very costly indeed.

In my opinion, animals kept for our consumption are reared in a deeply distressing way. Treated as foodstuffs while they are still alive, they are too often 'manufactured', stored and processed with little or no regard to dignity. There are many good, sensible and humane ways of farming animals which allow them freedom of movement, a sensible diet, sound health care and housing, and a quick death. Unfortunately for all of us, these methods are expensive and time consuming, like all organic farming.

Animals grow in the same way that we do, by obtaining building blocks from the foods they eat, and if their food is

THE HISTORY OF IT ALL

not good or does not supply the nutrients and roughage needed, then their flesh will not be good. Without the opportunity to exercise and metabolise waste products, they and other toxins build up in their systems without anywhere to go except into our meals. It horrifies me to think of people eating offal, in particular livers, where many of these toxins and other chemicals are deposited.

Organically-reared meats and poultry are now becoming available everywhere. These animals have all been fed organic produce, and will have been allowed to exercise regularly. They will not have been repeatedly exposed to disease-controlling drugs and massive doses of chemical wormers, growth enhancers, and the like. This means they are safe and fit to eat without providing any threat to our health. They also taste good.

The differences between fresh and farmed fish are harder to analyze. Fresh fish have the freedom to swim and eat where and what they like, although our seas and waterways are heavily polluted, so that may not be such an asset. Farmed fish are often kept in areas of water with poor drainage, and are fed colouring agents alongside a feeding regime aimed to fatten them as quickly as possible. Personally, I prefer fresh fish, and a friendly fishmonger who can tell you what area the fish comes from is a great help.

Animal flesh does not really feature in the detox diet until the final few days, so you may want to use the month ahead to seek out further information on these issues, and investigate your local food sources.

WATER

While not even loosely considered a food, the role of water in your diet is irreplaceable. You are 70 per cent water. Most of what you are is water-soluble. Many of the nutrients you need from your food are water-soluble. You can live for over 40 days without any food at all, but after just 24 hours without water your body is in trouble. It is very important to take the greatest care in the amount and quality of the water you drink while following the detox programme.

There was a warning on the news today to householders in the south-east of Britain. We were told to boil all drinking water, and in some areas it was cut off altogether. This was because some people had found small pink objects coming out of the taps along with their water. These were later identified as belonging to the shrimp family.

I am not convinced that water containing shrimps and other plankton is good for me. Nor is water which acts as a carrier and solvent for pesticides, that contains heavy metals and other toxic substances which the body often already has in excess.

Needless to say, I don't drink tap water. If you are lucky enough to live in an area where the tap water is good (and I don't think that would be anyone living in Britain), then drink tap water. Otherwise filter it, boil it, or drink bottled water.

Almost all water authorities in Britain exceed the maximum levels set by the European Commission for acceptable levels of lead in drinking water. Over 300 water authorities exceed the maximum levels for pesticides, and an estimated 2 million households are supplied with water containing unacceptably high levels of aluminium. In this country we add fluoride to our drinking water, whereas in every other country in Europe this practice has been banned because fluoride is believed to be a slow-acting poison.

If you are in any doubt, try these simple tests: drink only bottled water for one week, then try a glass of tap water. Your taste buds should be sufficiently rested to enable them to render a reliable response. Taste buds are one of the body's first lines of defence, but they can become jaded, and will adapt quickly to become enormously tolerant. One week on good clean water should be enough to sharpen them up again.

Try, too, making a cup of regular tea with boiled tap water, and another with boiled water that has been filtered first. Look into the cups — if your water supply is questionable, then one cup will be covered with a greasy scum, while the other will be clear. Following the idea of this programme to supply your body with fresh, pure materials, I think the extra scum could be done without.

Jug filters are readily available from department stores and health food shops, and I would recommend using one to filter all tap water used for cooking. For drinking I would recommend a good bottled water. There are now so many on the market, and they all taste different, and have different constitutions. Uncarbonated water is the best to drink through the detox programme, though you can have some 'fizzy' water — but look on it as a treat.

Always check the chemical composition of the water you choose — all bottles should have this printed on the label. You want to look for a high calcium to sodium ratio — more calcium than sodium — and no nitrates. As you will be drinking a lot of water, you may want to vary the brand. At this point, you might think that odd, but as your palate clears, and your system refines itself, you will soon find you can differentiate between the tastes of different brands.

One last word — if you choose a mineral water that comes in a plastic bottle, be very careful not to leave it in a warm place or in direct sunlight. If you do, the flavour of the water will be tainted by the plastic. Never buy a plastic bottle that has been in the window of a shop, or has been displayed under a bright spotlight.

4.
'YES' FOODS

Foods can be divided into families, types and groups. Food families are usually genetically related — rather like a family tree. Your cousins are part of your family, yet they almost certainly will have a separate household. The brassica family contains, among others, cauliflowers, broccoli and cabbage. They grow in different sites at different times of year, yet are all related to each other. Different types of food could be liquids and solids, or dried and fresh. Food groups are easily identifiable, for example, proteins, which include all animal flesh, and fats.

Every food, however, has its own individual chemical make-up. It is at this level that many active properties can be identified, and the differences between members of the same group, family or type become important.

If we look at cereals — corn, wheat, barley, rye, rice and so on — we find that wheat is much more acidic than corn; rice in its unrefined state contains more roughage than any of the others, and barley is highest in starch.

Further analysis allows specific substances to be isolated, and their benefits understood. It must be said that much of this analysis is aimed at enlarging our understanding, rather than promoting our health. Before we had laboratories with sophisticated equipment, we tried these foodstuffs out on ourselves. Our early ancestors naturally experimented with foods and herbs, seeking cures for their ills. Their findings were passed on through the generations, and form the bulk of our current knowledge. The nature of the healing properties of these remedies does not date, although they are sometimes little used.

This detox programme relies heavily on the active healing properties contained in specific foods. The foods themselves have been carefully selected, and the state in

'YES' FOODS

which they should be eaten is also important. We have already looked at how they are grown — what happens to foods once they are harvested or farmed has an enormous influence on their nutritional value.

Vitamins are divided into those that are soluble in water, and those that are fat-soluble. Cooking destroys many of the water-soluble vitamins, and there is often less nourishment to be found in a well-cooked cabbage, than in the water in which it was boiled. The fat-soluble vitamins cannot be well absorbed by the body if there is an absence of fat in the diet, or if there are any problems with fat metabolism.

Refining foods means discarding the parts which usually contain the bulk of the vitamins and minerals. In the production of white flour, the bran, germ and the outer coating of the wheat are discarded. This means that between 60 and 88 per cent of the B vitamins are either thrown away, or sold as cattle food.

When food is canned, vitamin C and many B vitamins are lost, the sodium/potassium balance is destroyed by added salt and, if aluminium is used for the can, there is a very real risk that this will be absorbed by the food while it is again heated and sealed.

I cannot stress enough the benefits that you will gain from eating fresh foods that are obtained from a reliable source. Your food should contain all the nutrients that it is supposed to have — all the nutrients that your body needs. It is your responsibility to nourish yourself well, and look after your health. Most people manage this expertly in terms of taking exercise, avoiding carcinogenic and harmful substances, and generally being good to themselves. You cannot afford to take your food supplies for granted, though, and once you have started to pay attention to this area of your life, you'll find it is not only rewarding, but remarkably simple to do.

SHORT-GRAIN BROWN RICE

Short-grain brown rice is a staple of the detox diet. It has a much larger surface area than its long-grain cousin, more

'YES' FOODS

B vitamins, and more fibre. It is broken down and digested much more easily and quickly, and its tremendous absorption means it will readily soak up all the toxins released into your gut.

The cellulose in the raw fruit and vegetables together with the extra water you will be drinking while you follow this programme will ensure a rapid movement of all this material out of your system.

Imagine a near empty jar of honey. Basically the jar is empty, but there is still a little honey left clinging to the sides. If you filled it up with water the contents would seem pretty murky. You could just keep pouring water into the jar and it would clean, but it would take a long time. Now imagine filling the jar with something that would absorb all the murky water, and could be tipped out, leaving no residue. Brown rice will leave your gut a clear and friendly place in which the bacteria that should be there may grow. This bacteria can then do their job of extracting maximum goodness out of your food.

Your digestive system is a little like a conveyor belt. Food passes along it and certain things need to happen to it in the right place, and in the right sequence. If you were making a car, you couldn't hang the doors until the body or frame was in place, and you couldn't top up the oil levels if the engine wasn't there. The end product with your digestion is not the final material, but the absorption that happens along the way, and if the operatives aren't at their stations to do their bit, then it all breaks down.

A congested bowel means that only a small percentage of nutrients can be absorbed. So, however much good food you are eating, you will not be able to benefit from it. Cleansing the whole digestive system makes maximum absorption possible, and means you will get the most from everything you eat.

SEA VEGETABLES

These may not be a regular part of your current diet, but they form an invaluable part of the detox programme. The iodine obtained from eating a very small amount of sea vegetable each day is tremendously beneficial in terms of speeding up your metabolism and maintaining a steady rate of detoxification.

There are many different varieties to choose from, and you can stick to one or two that you like, or vary them according to your taste. The most common sea vegetables, or seaweeds, are *kelp* — of which there are nearly one thousand varieties, *wakame* and *nori*. Despite the strange names, seaweed is possibly the oldest sea crop known to humans. The Romans, Greeks and Chinese used it not only as a food but also for its medicinal qualities.

Sea vegetables are on sale in most oriental and health food shops. They can be soaked and cut up to add to salad meals (*wakame* is one of the best kinds to treat this way), or sprinkled on to food. *Nori* is ideal for sprinkling, and can be bought in sheets that you crumble yourself, or in packets of ready-torn flakes. Directions for how best to treat these 'weeds' will be on the pack, but remember that for this month, you will be eating them raw.

CAYENNE AND GINGER

These spices should be eaten each day. They both have a stimulating effect on your digestive tract, serve to warm the system generally, and purify the blood. Too many spices can have an abrasive effect on the stomach and the gut, but eating a small amount of these each day will keep your system up and running, and encourage elimination through the skin. Ginger is widely used in India as the base for a cooling drink. It stimulates sweating, essential in such a hot climate. A pinch of cayenne can also encourage your body to mobilise its reserves of vitamin C. This is a wonderful first aid measure for colds.

GARLIC

Garlic is the most cleansing member of the onion family. Its antibiotic effect provides an important support while

'YES' FOODS

undertaking a detox plan. Known since ancient times as a blood cleanser, the ancient Egyptians are said to have brought it to the Mediterranean, from where its use has spread. It contains antiseptic substances which tone up the digestive system, reduces blood pressure and can help to clear mucus conditions and bronchitis. It is also widely used as an antidote for poisons, stings and bites. Eaten daily it will prove an important aid to the success of your month's work.

You can eat as much as you like but at least one clove every day.

Chewing on a bunch of fresh parsley after eating any garlic will instantly freshen your palate. Once garlic becomes a regular part of your diet, however, you will soon find it leaves little or no odour on your breath.

BEETROOT

This humble root vegetable is a liver tonic. As the part of your body that is going to be doing most work while you are detoxifying, your liver needs all the help it can get. Opening up good routes of elimination is important, as is not putting too great a load on this important organ, but beetroot is tremendously revitalising. It is easy to find raw beetroot — most greengrocers buy them raw and then cook them before selling. They are usually more than happy to keep a few aside. As they go out of season, or if you do not like the flavour too well, there are now good beetroot juices on the market. These are available from health food shops and some supermarkets. Have some every day and your liver will thank you.

One word of warning: the sudden introduction of raw beetroot or beetroot juice to your diet may cause your urine to turn red. This is nothing to be alarmed about, and will cause you no harm. A friend of mine was so upset by this one evening that she drove to her local hospital. Seven months pregnant, she was seen straight away, and only when the doctor calmly asked her what she had eaten that day did the penny drop.

'YES' FOODS

SPROUTS

With an emphasis on filling the body with vitality, foods which support this aim are imperative. Sprouting turns a dead food into a live one. Tremendously rich in vitamins and minerals, sprouting can increase the vitamin content of some beans by up to 500 per cent! They also contain a higher level of protein and amino acids than many vegetables and current research points to them being an important source of vitamin B12. This would make them an essential part of any vegetarian or vegan diet.

You can sprout just about anything, and will find a wide variety in health food shops and on supermarket shelves; but they are remarkably easy to do for yourself at home, and a lot cheaper. You can buy a sprouter, or just use a glass jar. First rinse the seeds or beans and put them in the jar, covering it with a piece of muslin or cheesecloth or even some kitchen towel, and secure with a rubber band. Rinse at least twice a day with warm water, and leave the jar on its side to drain. Within about three days you should have a jar full of tasty, nutritious sprouts. It is well worth experimenting with different types, and varying the flavour of your salads.

Sprouted alfalfa was called the 'father of all foods' by ancient Arabs. It has a centuries-old reputation as a nutritious, appetite-enhancing, vitality-supporting food. It is one of the best dietary sources of chlorophyll, which is essential for wound repair, and has proven anti-infectious activity. More recently, alfalfa has been used as a spleen tonic, and for its role in reducing blood cholesterol. At the same time it is reputed to improve the clotting ability of blood and have an anti-rheumatic effect, thus helping in all arthritic conditions.

All these attributes are due to the complex nature of alfalfa, and the various important substances it contains. Alongside an assortment of vitamins, minerals, trace elements and amino acids, it is rich in the active properties of saponins and alkaloids.

'YES' FOODS

JUICES

Household juicers can be bought from any electrical store. Juicing is a wonderfully easy way to get maximum goodness from fruits and vegetables, and add variety to your diet.

Juices have an important role in any healthcare plan. They can speed up detoxification dramatically, and provide a revitalising rest for your digestive system. They are not essential to this detox programme, but can have a very positive effect upon it.

Many people find it difficult to eat early in the morning. This is largely due to a sluggish system that takes a long time to get into gear each day. Although sitting down to a dish of food may be daunting, the prospect of a sweet and refreshing drink is very appealing.

With the success of your programme, your system will soon be wanting breakfast every morning, as your body asks for energy to face the day ahead. At this point, juices can add to the variety of your early morning menu.

Throughout the day, too, juices can be substituted for a meal, or provide a simple, healthy snack. Juicing is the quickest way to prepare food, and can transform humble ingredients into a real treat.

Juices are not specific to your detox plan — they can form part of your everyday diet, as a quick pick-me-up, or an occasional 24-hour alternative to solid food.

You can juice just about anything, from apples to zucchini. I recommend never juicing garlic, though, as the pungent taste will take ages to shift. When I got my first juicer, I experimented with all sorts of things, had many successes and a few terrible mistakes, the most marked of which was juicing garlic. Every other juice I had that week tasted of garlic, and that was after I had soaked the juicer overnight and cleaned and scrubbed it as hard as I could.

Some juice combinations are included in the recipe sections. I hope they will whet your appetite and encourage you to try them. These juices do not need to be diluted with water, unlike commercial juices, because much of the flesh and fibre of the fruit or vegetable will still be present.

5.
'NO' FOODS

In much the same way as some foods promote good health, some others can place a burden on the body. There are some specific foods you will not be able to eat while your body is detoxifying, and some of these may come as a bit of a surprise.

I think we all know the sense in avoiding powerful, artificial stimulants. Caffeine is most certainly one of these. Present in teas as well as coffee, its effects can include anxiety, insomnia and high blood pressure. When you have a cup of coffee, your blood sugar level is instantly raised, and your adrenal glands (responsible for 'fight or flight' energy messages) go into overdrive. At this point there is usually no external physical crisis to react to, so your system crashes. When this happens, you feel low and in need of another lift — often another cup of coffee. Does this sound familiar?

The internal effects of this continuous, erratic loading up and down are devastating — depleting energy reserves and confusing kidney function. I knew a very heavy coffee drinker who just wanted to sleep for two days after giving it up. He was so overtired and worn down by the constant on/off messages from the caffeine that his system was exhausted. This is an extreme case — he drank pints of real coffee every day — but it illustrates the point.

Drinking decaffeinated coffee is not the answer. The chemicals used in the process of extracting the caffeine are not desirable either. Recent research has also linked coffee drinking to high blood cholesterol levels, and both real and instant coffee are implicated. Some coffees are decaffeinated by using a water extraction method. Although this means that the heavy chemical content is avoided, heating can compound the cholesterol threat.

'NO' FOODS

Some foods we just eat too much of. In the West, we have adopted wheat as our dietary staple, with painful consequences. Although wheat has been eaten for more than 9,000 years, its place in our diet has changed considerably — as has the wheat itself. What we eat today bears little resemblance to the wheat our forbears grew. Structurally altered, the product of plant husbandry and selective strain breeding, this cereal is often treated as a toxin by our digestive enzymes and our immune systems.

Its role as an aggravator in arthritic conditions has recently been confirmed, and for years it has been regarded as mucus-forming and irritating to the digestive tract. Most healthy people can tolerate some wheat and extract some benefits from it. Among other things, if eaten in its unrefined or 'whole' state it is rich in B vitamins. The problems start when wheat or wheat-based flour is eaten all the time — toast for breakfast, a sandwich at lunch, perhaps a biscuit in the afternoon and pasta for supper. We have found so many uses for this versatile grain. It is found as a filler in some meat dishes, is used as a thickener for sauces, a base for desserts, and slips into almost every meal in one or another of its guises.

Whenever a food is eaten extensively, to the exclusion of other members of its family, the seeds of allergy are sown. There are so many other grains to choose from — like rice, rye, millet and barley — that there is no need to feel any deprivation or loss if you eliminate wheat as a staple. Throughout this month, wheat is eliminated entirely, and I would suggest it should be handled with great care thereafter.

I would recommend taking a good look at your present diet before starting the detox plan. If there is any food that holds a regular, essential position in your everyday life, then it could be an allergen. I have seen countless examples of this, even with seemingly innocent foods.

If you are in any way addicted to a food, if you feel better for eating it, then I suggest you view it with suspicion. If it is one of the foods included in this detox plan, eliminate it anyway. Put it on your list of foods to try when

'NO' FOODS

you finish the programme, and see how you react. It may be fine, but you will not have suffered by avoiding it for a month, and you can only gain if it can be reintroduced to your diet in more manageable quantities.

We tend to think of all fruits and vegetables as being health-giving foods. This is basically true, yet when we look to their chemical composition, we can find some unusual facts.

Tomatoes, spinach, rhubarb and sorrel all contain large amounts of oxalic acid. Apart from being very corrosive and irritating to the gut, they are very acidic and can be involved in blocking the uptake of calcium. This makes it extremely important for women to look closely at this food group. Under normal circumstances, they may not trouble you at all, although this is one of the major food groups indicated in disturbances such as migraine and some arthritic conditions.

On this programme you are eliminating as many possible aggravators as possible, and while your system is fighting hard to expel all impurities, any 'suspect' foods must be eliminated.

Avocados and bananas have high starch and fat contents along with *peanuts* (which are actually a pulse, and not a nut) and *coconut* (the hardest fat of all for your body to deal with). Although they are filling, they will slow up your rate of absorption and the movement of foods through your intestines. Avocados and bananas also contain vaso-active amines which, if you have a sensitivity to them, can dampen some of the positive effects of your circulation-enhancing exercises.

Lentils are excluded because whatever you do to them, they seem to cause gas. However quickly they are moved through the body, they have this effect. One of the biggest changes you will experience after this month is a mammoth lift in energy levels, and this is to a great extent due to the changes that will have taken place in your gut. Apart from being cleansed, your bowel will have been reinstating a colony of beneficial bacteria, and ousting any harmful substances. Any interruption of this process, due

'NO' FOODS

to excess gas for instance, can only slow things down.

Mushrooms are not a true vegetable, but a fungus. Many of the nutrients from your food are actually absorbed into the body via the bowel. This absorption, along with other important functions, is reliant upon the help of 'friendly' bacteria. The eco-balance of your gut is a complicated one, but simply put, overgrowths of other bacteria and fungus can interfere with this delicate balance.

Severe overgrowths of unfriendly bacteria are often what is referred to when people talk of *candida*, and to tackle this problem requires specialist care. The flora and fauna of most people's intestines, however, could often have their ratios improved, and this detoxification plan will redress any minor imbalances.

The positive effects of beetroot on your liver have been described above. *Oranges* are the absolute opposite. They and their juice have a debilitating, congesting effect on the liver. They should be avoided completely throughout your detox month, and treated with care thereafter. The idea that they are a good source of vitamin C and therefore valuable in your diet is total fallacy. Once the orange has been picked, artificially ripened, refrigerated, shipped and stored, only the smallest amount of any active vitamin could hope to survive. Oranges are also the most acidic of all citrus fruits, and should not be given to children.

6. YOUR DETOX PLAN

Looking through the next few pages you will see how simple and straightforward the detox diet is. You should by now be convinced that it is well worth beginning and be looking forward to getting started. All the whys and wherefores are explained, together with a selection of the questions I'm most often asked by people embarking on their month's detox.

Stick closely to the eating plan. Read through it a few times to make sure everything is quite clear — you might like to make up your next shopping list at the same time. It is quite a good idea to make a note of some of the particulars in your diary, or to use a sticker or post-it note on your refrigerator or larder door. This is particularly useful if others in your household will not be following the programme along with you. While not doubting your resolve in any way, one of the commonest causes of breaking the diet plan is simple forgetfulness. This is very easy in the beginning if you are involved in preparing meals for others.

The diet plan is split into three stages:

Stage I Days 1–3 Transition
Stage II Days 4–25 Main Detox
Stage III Days 26–30 Introduction to a regular diet

The first three days are the toughest of the whole month, and when you look at the food plan you will see a marked change between Stages I and II. For Stage I you will be eating a restricted range of foods which are specifically designed to give you as much support as possible. They will allow your digestive system to rest, and provide a gentle introduction to detoxification.

This first stage is tough because your body will be starting to detoxify and its means of elimination will be neither adequately established, nor sufficiently clear.

It is during this time (and usually on the third day) that you will encounter a healing crisis. This usually takes the form of a mild headache or a drop in appetite, accompanied by a change of mood. This is the time when any particular symptoms such as a poor skin, or a sinus condition may worsen, or you may see the recurrence of an old health problem like a chesty cough, or cold.

This is all transitional, and these physical symptoms are usually over by the next day, although you may wake with a coated tongue or a dry throat.

This is the time too, when cravings may appear. You might be expecting to miss coffee or chocolate, but any cravings are often for more surprising foods, like bread, bananas, cereal or pasta. If your diet has been high in caffeine — from soft drinks, chocolate, tea and coffee — then this withdrawal period is also likely to make you rather tired and listless, enhancing the feelings, in fact, that would make you desire another caffeine boost.

The healing crisis is a positive sign. Essentially, it is proof that your body is strong enough and has enough vitality to clear itself out. The symptoms are a sign of the accumulated impurities being pushed out of your body, leaving it ready to resume healthy, normal living. Once you are over this third day hump, it gets easier and easier. You will notice a return to energy levels you forgot were possible!

Vital to the ease and success of this first stage are your back-up measures of skin brushing, water paddling and exercise. The faster you can encourage your body to eliminate, the easier the transition to full detoxification.

The second stage of this programme is a solid, two-pronged move towards better health. You are supplying energy and vitality to your body with every meal, while at the same time encouraging your eliminative channels to rid it of pollutants. This lasts for three weeks, enabling a turnover of your immune system. (Like every other part of your body, your immune system has a cycle of rest and regeneration.)

It is during Stage II that you will notice the more dramatic changes. Your weight will alter, dropping initially and then finding its own comfortable level. If weight loss is necessary, this will continue at a steady rate throughout the programme. Otherwise, your weight will settle after about the first week.

You will have more time, and more energy to use in that time. A spring will appear in your step, and you'll notice your breathing is clearer. Your sense of smell will sharpen, as will your other senses. Most people find their powers of thought are clearer, and they have speedier reaction times.

Your skin will be clear and softer than before, and your posture will improve as your chest opens and your physical confidence increases.

Most important, though, is an indefinable feeling of overall well-being. Life becomes easier because you have the energy resource to meet daily challenges, and the ability to fully appreciate life's beauty.

At the end of Stage II, just when you are beginning to get bored with the diet, you can expect an emotional clear-out. This will take your mind off food, and switch it to other areas which may need attention. Many people find they have a tearful day, or an angry or depressed day right at the end of the main detox.

Just as the physical healing crisis you will have experienced earlier was short-term, so is this — seldom lasting longer than 24 hours. It can, however, supply you with valuable personal insights in that time, and is extremely important.

Stage III will see you reintroducing a wider range of cooked foods, and preparing yourself for a return to everyday life. This section is carefully controlled to enable you to make a smooth return to a wider diet with specially selected meals and a day-by-day dietary guide.

Do not be tempted to skip this stage — it can be

YOUR DETOX PLAN

tempting when you are so close to completing the programme — but it is important to take things slowly. Your entire body has been involved in a dynamic spring clean, and will not be ready or able to assimilate a heavy meal that is full of unusual foods at this time. Besides, you will be fully satisfied by the food plan that is provided, as you slowly encourage your body to deal with a wide variety of nutrient sources.

You may even find things moving a bit too quickly for you. If that happens, it simply means that your body is not yet ready for more cooked foods. You can extend this stage to cover about two weeks — just introduce one new type of food every few days. Let your body guide you, and don't force yourself to eat something you don't want just because it is on the daily plan.

I recommend you take a full spectrum multi-vitamin and mineral supplement throughout this detox programme, and for about four weeks afterwards. This is so that any long-term deficiencies can be put to rights, and it will also provide additional support for your detoxification. Taking it for four weeks after you have completed the programme is important because it can take that long for you to 'top up' on some of these essential nutrients.

Always take your supplements with meals to obtain the maximum benefit from them, and to make it easier for your digestion.

You get what you pay for with dietary supplements, so don't be tempted to buy the cheapest ones you can find. If you are in doubt, consult a naturopath or dietary therapist, and they will recommend some for you. You need to buy a supplement with a contents list that includes all the following: Vitamin A, B1, B2, B3, B5, B6, B12, C, D3 (cholecalciferol) and E; Choline, Inositol, PABA, Iodine, Calcium, Chromium, Iron, Magnesium, Manganese, Molybdenum, Potassium, Selenium, Zinc and Bioflavonoids.

Check the other ingredients to make sure there is no added wheat, sugar, yeast, artificial colour, preservative or colouring. (You may be surprised — one vitamin C

YOUR DETOX PLAN

supplement I saw recently had sugar as its main ingredient, and orange colouring and flavouring a little further down the list.)

Depending on how these tablets are made, you may find your urine taking on a green or orange hue. This is nothing to be alarmed about, and is just your body's eliminative route for any excess B vitamins (if your urine looks orange) or the tabletting additives of parsley, watercress, alfalfa and the like (if it takes on a greenish hue).

Your body stores many vitamins and minerals, but some, like vitamin C, need replenishing almost every day. It is very important not to stop taking your supplement suddenly, but to lower the dose, and slowly phase it out. If you are taking three tablets a day, for instance, drop to two a day for about a week, then one a day, and one every other day, until you run out. Stopping suddenly can be a very real shock to your system, and risks undoing some of the hard work you will have put in throughout the detox programme.

7.
STAGE I

Follow this eating plan for days 1–3 of your detox programme.

- Drink at least 1.5 litres (2½ pints) of water each day
- Eat at least 3 meals a day — breakfast is a MUST
- Do not drink anything with meals or for half an hour afterwards
- Start each day with a glass of lemon water
- Have your final meal of the day before 8 p.m.

BREAKFAST

Choose from:

- Any dried fruit that has been soaked in water overnight
- Any uncooked, fresh fruit from this list:

apple	lime
apricot	lychee
cherry	mango
date	nectarine
fig	papaya
grape	peach
grapefruit	pear
guava	persimmon
kiwi	pineapple
kumquat	pomegranate
lemon	star fruit

You can eat melons, but do not mix them with any other fruit.

- Any raw seeds, e.g. sunflower, sesame, pumpkin
- Live goat's or sheep's yoghurt

STAGE I

You can eat as much or as little as you like, and pick any combination of foods. Once you have had breakfast, you can continue to eat any of the above foods as snacks until noon.

LUNCH AND DINNER

- Boiled short-grain brown rice
- Any vegetables from this list, steamed or cooked using the low water method:
  asparagus
  beetroot
  broccoli
  cabbage (white, red and green)
  carrot
  cauliflower
  celery
  courgette
  Chinese leaves
  green beans
  leeks
  mangetout
  onions (all types)
  parsnips
  peas
  swede
  sweetcorn or corn on the cob
  spring greens
  turnip

- 1 small salad comprising any fresh raw foods from this list:
  basil
  celeriac
  chayote
  chicory
  chives
  cress
  cucumber

daikon (giant white radish)
dandelion leaves
dill
endive
fennel
garlic
ginger
lamb's lettuce
lettuce
lollo rosso
nettle
parsley
radicchio
radish
rosemary
sage
tarragon
thyme
watercress

Dress the salad with olive, safflower, sunflower or sesame seed oil and lemon juice.

Ideally each meal will be of rice and steamed vegetables with a small salad. If preferred, you could have rice and salad at one meal and rice with steamed vegetables for the other.

You can have any herbal teas throughout the day, but no fruit tea.

RECIPES

Lemon water
Place a slice of lemon, or a squeeze of fresh lemon juice in a mug. Cover with a little cold water and top up with boiling water.

Boiled brown rice
The secret of light, fluffy rice is not to disturb it whilst cooking. Choose a saucepan with a tight fitting lid, and do

STAGE I

not be tempted to lift the lid to check how the rice is cooking. Above all, do not stir it. Brown rice takes longer to cook than refined white rice.

This will make enough for 2 servings. You could increase the amount of rice and water proportionately, and make enough for future meals. Cooked brown rice can be stored, covered, in a fridge for up to two days.

2½ cups water
1 cup brown rice

Bring the measured water to the boil in a saucepan with a close-fitting lid. Rinse the rice well until the water runs clear, and add it to the boiling water. Return to the boil and skim off any scum with a spoon. Cover the pan, and reduce the heat to a gentle simmer. The rice should be cooked after 35 minutes. Rinse it through with boiling water before serving.

Low water cooking
This is a good alternative to steaming, and any vegetables can be cooked this way.

450g (1lb) mixed vegetables
5–6 large lettuce leaves
2 tablespoons water

Chop a selection of vegetables into small pieces or thin slices. Line a saucepan with the rinsed lettuce leaves. Add the vegetables to the pan with the water. Bring to the boil watching carefully, because you will hardly see the water. Cover with a tight fitting lid and turn down the heat immediately. Simmer gently for 3–5 minutes.

Live muesli
225g (8oz) mixed dried fruit, soaked overnight
1 unpeeled apple, chopped
1 unpeeled pear, chopped
handful of cherries, stoned
small bunch of grapes, with seeds
120ml (4floz) live goat's or sheep's yoghurt
1 tablespoon sesame seeds

1 tablespoon sunflower seeds
1 teaspoon poppy seeds

Drain the dried fruit and place in a bowl. Add the chopped apple, pear and cherries and blend together. Halve the grapes and add them to the fruit mixture. Cover with the yoghurt and sprinkle with the sesame, sunflower and poppy seeds.

Dried fruit salad
50g (2oz) dried peaches
225g (8oz) dried apricots
125g (4oz) dried prunes
50g (2oz) dried figs
50g (2oz) split almonds
50g (2oz) pine nuts
50g (2oz) sunflower seeds
1 tablespoon rose water
seeds from 3 cardamom pods

Wash all the fruits and place them in a large bowl. Mix in the nuts and seeds and just cover with water. Sprinkle over the rose water and cardamom seeds. Let the fruits soak for at least 6 hours or overnight. Much of the liquid will be absorbed, the remainder serves as a lovely syrup.

Juice Suggestions
A juice extractor is really necessary for these recipes, although some soft fruit combinations can also be prepared successfully with a food processor or blender.

My favourite breakfast juice
1 large slice pineapple
2 apples
1 pear
1 slice lemon
small bunch of grapes
150ml (5floz) live goat's or sheep's yoghurt

Peel the pineapple slice, and core the apples and pear. Pass *all* the fruit through the juicer and then whisk in the yoghurt for a smooth, creamy and satisfying meal in a glass.

Summer juice treat
Juice 1 peach with 2 apples, a small punnet of strawberries, 3 apricots and 1 nectarine.

Tropical juice
Juice 2 apples with the flesh of 1 mango and 1 kiwi fruit and a quarter of a papaya.

Thirst quencher
Juice half a pineapple with 2 grapefruit.

Sandra's special
Juice half an unpeeled cucumber with 2 carrots, 1 lettuce heart and then whisk in 250ml (8floz) live goat's or sheep's yoghurt.

8.
STAGE II

Follow this eating plan for days 4–25 of your detox programme.

- Start each day with a glass of lemon water
- Drink at least 1.5 litres (2½ pints) of water each day
- Eat at least 3 meals — breakfast is a MUST
- Do not drink with meals or for half an hour afterwards
- Do not eat after 8 p.m.
- Every day, have:
  1 portion raw beetroot or 1 glass beetroot juice
  1 small piece of fresh ginger
  1 teaspoon cayenne pepper
  1 teaspoon/sheet/strand sea vegetable (depending on type)
  1 serving alfalfa sprouts
  1 clove raw garlic

BREAKFAST

Choose from:

- Any uncooked, fresh fruit from this list:

apple	guava
apricot	kiwi
bilberry	kumquat
blackcurrant	lemon
blueberry	lime
cherry	loganberry
cranberry	lychee
date	mango
fig	nectarine
grape	papaya
grapefruit	passion fruit
greengage	peach

STAGE II

>   pear
>   persimmon
>   pineapple
>   plantain
>   pomegranate
>   quince
>   redcurrant
>   satsuma
>   star fruit
>   strawberry
>   tangerine
>
>   But NO BANANA, ORANGE, COCONUT OR RHUBARB.
>   You can eat melons, but do not mix them with other fruits.
>
> - Any raw seeds, e.g. sunflower, poppy, pumpkin, sesame, anise, caraway.
> - Live goat's or sheep's yoghurt.

You can eat as much as you like, and pick any combination of foods. Once you have eaten breakfast, you can continue to eat any of these foods as snacks until noon.

LUNCH AND DINNER

- Boiled short-grain brown rice (see page 38)
- Any uncooked, unsalted nuts, e.g. almond, brazil, cashew, hazelnut, pine nut, pecan, walnut
  BUT NO PEANUTS
- Any sprouted beans, seeds or peas, e.g. alfalfa, chick pea, fenugreek, mung, bamboo, wheat berry
  BUT NO LENTILS
- Any fresh herbs, e.g. basil, dill, marjoram, rosemary, sage, tarragon, thyme
  BUT NO SORREL
- Any goat's or sheep's cheese
- Any live goat's or sheep's yoghurt
- Olive and any seed oils, e.g. sunflower, sesame
- Freshly squeezed lemon and lime juice
- Any herbal tea except those containing orange fruit or extract
- Any fruit juice except orange, diluted 50/50 with water
- Any vegetable juice from your list diluted half and half with water
  BUT NO TOMATO OR SPINACH

STAGE II

- Any raw vegetables from this list:
  artichoke
  asparagus
  beet greens
  beetroot
  broccoli
  Brussels sprouts
  cabbage (white, red and green)
  carrot
  cauliflower
  celeriac
  celery
  chard
  chayote
  chicory
  Chinese leaves
  chives
  collard
  courgette
  cress
  cucumber
  daikon (giant white radish)
  dandelion leaves
  dulse
  endive
  fennel
  green beans
  green peas
  kale
  kohlrabi
  leeks
  lettuce
  lollo rosso
  mangetout
  okra (ladies fingers)
  onions (all types)
  parsley
  parsnip
  peppers (all types)

STAGE II

potato
radish
saladings
spring greens
swede
sweetcorn or corn on the cob
sweet potato
turnip
watercress
BUT NO TOMATO, AVOCADO, SPINACH OR MUSHROOMS

RECIPES

The following recipes and unusual combinations of foods are really just a taster of what is possible. Throughout, the oils used are olive, sunflower or sesame, and these can be interchanged according to your own taste. Wherever cheese is mentioned it is goat's or sheep's, and all the yoghurt is live goat's or sheep's.

Wherever possible, do not peel fruits and vegetables. Most of their vitamins and minerals lie just below the skin, and it is often one of the tastiest parts, so only peel if you are using non-organic produce and are worried about wax coatings or pesticide residues.

It is always difficult to judge portion sizes, as we all have our own ideas on this, so the quantities used in the following recipes are meant only as a guide. They can all be stored in a fridge or larder, so I suggest you play with the amounts, perhaps making enough for more than one day at a time, until you develop your own favourites.

Those recipes marked with an asterisk * are not only suitable for entertaining, but rather impressive too.

Dressings

Basil
Combine 1 sprig fresh basil, 1 crushed clove of garlic and 1 handful of chopped parsley with 6 tablespoons of oil and 2–3 tablespoons of lemon juice. Add a sprig of tarragon.

Basil and pine nut
Mix together 1 sprig of fresh basil with 50g (2oz) of crushed pine nuts, 1 crushed clove of garlic, 2–3 tablespoons of lemon juice and 6 tablespoons of olive oil.

Both these recipes make quite large amounts. If all is not used at one meal, they will keep for up to one week if stored in a screwtop jar in the fridge. Storing makes for a stronger flavour, too, so you may want to make larger amounts of a selection of dressings.

Coriander
Add leaf coriander and chopped parsley to a basic mixture of lime juice, crushed garlic cloves, olive oil and sesame oil, varying the amounts to taste.

Yoghurt
Using live sheep's or goat's yoghurt as a base, add chopped fresh mint, cucumber and crushed garlic.

Yoghurt crumble
Mix a little crumbled goat's or sheep's cheese with live yoghurt, adding crushed garlic and chopped cucumber to taste.

Green yoghurt
Combine shredded watercress with live goat's or sheep's yoghurt and chopped mint. Add whichever fresh green herbs are to hand.

Fennel
Finely chop green pepper and fennel root, add garlic to taste and combine with olive oil and lemon juice.

Courgette
Combine grated courgette with lemon juice and olive oil, adding cumin seeds and garlic or mint to taste.

STAGE II

Soups

Cold summer soup
1 large cucumber, coarsely chopped
1 tablespoon freshly chopped mint
600 ml (1 pint) live goat's or sheep's yoghurt
600 ml (1 pint) water
50 g (2 oz) walnuts, chopped
2 spring onions, chopped

Place the cucumber and mint in a food processor or blender with the yoghurt and water and work to a purée. Transfer to individual serving bowls and garnish with the walnuts and spring onions.
Serves 6

Creamed almond soup
50 g (2 oz) ground almonds
1 teaspoon coriander seeds
1 tablespoon freshly chopped basil
1 teaspoon freshly chopped thyme
300 ml (½ pint) live goat's or sheep's yoghurt
1.2 litres (2 pints) water
1 teaspoon lemon rind
1 tablespoon split almonds, to garnish

Place the ground almonds, coriander seeds, basil and thyme in a food processor or blender with the yoghurt and water. Work until thoroughly blended. Add the lemon rind and leave to stand for at least 20 minutes. Work the mixture a second time. Transfer to individual serving bowls and sprinkle over split almonds to garnish.
Serves 4–6

Summer borscht
1 carrot, grated
1 onion, chopped
675 g (1½ lb) raw beetroot, grated
1.2 litres (2 pints) water
juice of 1 lemon
To garnish:
3 tablespoons live goat's or sheep's yoghurt

3 teaspoons freshly chopped coriander
3 teaspoons freshly chopped parsley
Place the carrot, onion and beetroot in a liquidiser or food processor with the water and lemon juice. Work until thoroughly blended. Transfer to individual serving bowls and garnish with swirls of yoghurt and finely chopped coriander and parsley.
Serves 6

Salad Combinations

Broccoli and ginger
125g (4oz) broccoli florets
25g (1oz) chopped almonds
1 spring onion, finely chopped
1" square fresh ginger, peeled and finely chopped
1 tablespoon olive oil
1 clove garlic, crushed or chopped
Break the broccoli florets into small sprigs. Place them in a bowl with the almonds and chopped onion and mix lightly together. Combine the olive oil with the garlic and pour this dressing over the salad. Toss lightly before serving.

Red and white coleslaw
½ red cabbage, finely shredded
½ white cabbage, finely shredded
1 stick celery, chopped
2 spring onions, finely chopped
1 large apple, cored and chopped
25g (1oz) walnuts
25g (1oz) almonds
1 tablespoon freshly chopped coriander
1 tablespoon freshly chopped parsley
25g (1oz) sunflower seeds, to garnish
For the dressing:
150ml (5floz) live goat's or sheep's yoghurt
2 teaspoons lemon juice
1 teaspoon grated lemon rind
1 clove garlic, chopped

STAGE II

1 tablespoon freshly chopped parsley
1 tablespoon freshly chopped chives

In a large bowl combine the red and white cabbage with the chopped celery and onion. Add the apple, nuts and herbs and combine evenly. Place all the ingredients for the dressing in a small bowl and beat together to form a smooth mixture. Pour the dressing over the coleslaw and toss to coat the ingredients. Sprinkle with the sunflower seeds and serve.

Sesame cabbage
125 g (4 oz) green cabbage, shredded
2 tablespoons sesame seeds
½ tablespoon sesame oil
1 teaspoon lemon juice

Place the cabbage in a bowl. Combine the sesame oil, lemon juice and sesame seeds in a small bowl or screwtop jar. Pour over the cabbage and toss well in the dressing. Serve immediately.

Cabbage, thyme and feta crumble
½ cabbage
8 green olives, stoned and halved
50 g (2 oz) feta cheese, crumbled
2 tablespoons olive oil
1 tablespoon lemon juice
1 teaspoon freshly chopped thyme leaves

Slice the cabbage thinly and arrange it on a plate. Strew the olives and feta cheese on top. Dress with the mixed olive oil and lemon juice, then sprinkle over the thyme, rubbing the leaves between your fingers to release the full flavour.

Carrot and daikon
1 carrot, grated
1 daikon (giant white radish), grated
1 spring onion, finely sliced
1 tablespoon sesame seeds
1 tablespoon sesame oil

1 teaspoon lemon juice
a few parsley sprigs, to garnish

Combine all the ingredients, except the parsley, in a large bowl and leave to stand for at least 30 minutes for the flavours to combine. Serve garnished with parsley sprigs for colour.

Carrot with garlic, ginger and cumin
1 large carrot, grated
1 teaspoon cumin seeds, crushed
1 teaspoon lemon or lime juice
1 clove garlic, crushed
1 teaspoon grated root ginger

Mix all the ingredients together in a bowl. Leave to stand for 1 hour before serving to allow the carrot to become imbued with the flavour of the ginger and cumin seeds.

*Cauliflower coated with cheese**
1 small cauliflower
8 tablespoons olive oil
juice of 1 lemon
125 g (4 oz) feta cheese
3–4 tablespoons live goat's or sheep's yoghurt
4 tablespoons sesame seeds

Break the cauliflower into small florets. Place in a glass or porcelain dish and pour over the combined oil and lemon juice. Leave to marinate for at least 1½ hours. Remove the cauliflower from the marinade with a slotted spoon, reserving the liquid. Arrange the cauliflower in a serving dish.

Crumble the feta cheese into enough yoghurt to give a nice coating consistency. Spoon this mixture over the cauliflower and sprinkle with sesame seeds.

The reserved marinade can be refrigerated and used as a base for other salad dressings.

Celery sticks filled with feta
2 sticks celery
50 g (2 oz) feta cheese
1 teaspoon freshly chopped mint

STAGE II

1–2 teaspoons live goat's or sheep's yoghurt (optional)

Place the feta in a small bowl and, using a fork, combine it with the mint. Add a little yoghurt if it makes the mixture easier to work with. Cut the celery sticks into 7.5cm (3 inch) lengths, and fill each one with the cheese and mint mixture.

*Celery bundles**

2 sticks celery
3 tablespoons olive oil
1 teaspoon lemon juice
1 large red chilli pepper
a small bunch of chives

Cut the celery into 5cm (2 inch) lengths, then into fine julienne strips. Place in a glass or porcelain dish and pour over the combined oil and lemon juice. Leave to marinate for up to 1 hour. Meanwhile, slice the chilli into fine rings cross-wise, discarding all the seeds. Slot the strips of celery through the pepper rings (one by one is easiest) until it holds them in a bundle. Tie these into larger bundles using the chives.

Carrots and courgettes can also be used, for variety, using green chilli peppers to bind them, with strips of seaweed to tie into larger bundles.

Note: After touching chilli peppers, wash your hands immediately. Do not touch your eyes or lips.

Chicory and fennel in coriander dressing

1 head chicory, finely chopped
1 head fennel, finely chopped
1 lettuce heart, finely chopped
a bunch of coriander leaves, shredded

For the dressing:
120ml (4 fl oz) olive oil
3 teaspoons lemon juice
1 teaspoon crushed coriander seeds

Place the chicory, fennel, lettuce and shredded coriander in a serving bowl. Mix lightly together. Place the ingredients for the dressing in a screwtop jar and shake vigorously to combine. Pour over the salad, toss lightly and serve.

Chayote with basil and pumpkin seeds
1 chayote, diced
1 tablespoon pumpkin seeds
For the dressing:
1 tablespoon olive oil
1 teaspoon lemon juice
1 tablespoon freshly chopped basil
1 clove garlic, crushed or chopped
1 carrot, shredded, to garnish

Combine the chayote and pumpkin seeds in a serving bowl. Blend the dressing ingredients together in a small bowl or screwtop jar and pour over the chayote. Toss well to coat, and serve immediately, garnished with shredded carrot.

*Celery and goat's cheese wheels**
225g (8oz) goat's cheese
approximately 4 tablespoons live goat's or sheep's yoghurt
1 tablespoon finely chopped chives
2 tablespoons finely chopped walnuts
1 small head celery

In a small bowl, combine the goat's cheese with enough yoghurt to make a pliable mixture. Add the finely chopped chives and walnuts. Trim and wash the celery, being careful to keep it in one piece. Keep some of the nicest leaves for a garnish. Open the head of celery carefully and fill it with the cheese mixture. Wrap tightly in a plasticizer-free cling film and refrigerate for about 2 hours or until the filling is firm. Unwrap the celery and cut it across in slices with a sharp knife. Arrange on a serving platter, garnished with the reserved celery leaves.

Courgette and leeks with feta and yoghurt
1 courgette, trimmed
1 leek, trimmed and well-washed
1 teaspoon ground cumin

25 g (1 oz) feta cheese, crumbled
For the dressing:
1 tablespoon live goat's or sheep's yoghurt
1 teaspoon lemon juice
1 tablespoon olive oil
1 tablespoon freshly chopped mint

Thinly slice the courgette and leek and place in a serving bowl. Strew over the ground cumin and the cheese. Combine the ingredients for the dressing in a small bowl and pour over the salad. Toss lightly to coat the vegetables and serve.

*Cucumber Cups**
1 cucumber
175 g (6 oz) feta cheese, crumbled
120 ml (4 fl oz) live goat's or sheep's yoghurt
1 carrot, washed and trimmed
1 green pepper, cored and deseeded
1 yellow pepper, cored and deseeded
fresh mint leaves, to garnish

Cut the cucumber into 5 cm (2 inch) lengths. Scoop out most of the flesh from each piece leaving a cup shape with a small base. Combine the feta and yoghurt and use this mixture to fill each 'cup'. Cut the carrot and peppers into fine strips and place a few of each upright in the cucumber cups. Garnish with fresh mint leaves.

*Endive boats**
6 large, crisp endive leaves
125 g (4 oz) feta cheese, crumbled
4 tablespoons live goat's or sheep's yoghurt
2 tablespoons crushed walnuts

Arrange the endive leaves on a serving platter. Combine the cheese, yoghurt and walnuts in a small bowl, stirring well. Spoon this mixture into the endive leaves, dividing it equally between them. Serve immediately.

Endive with tarragon
125 g (4 oz) endive, roughly chopped

1 tablespoon shredded tarragon leaves
mixed salad leaves, washed and shredded
1 red pepper, cored, deseeded and cut into strips
1 yellow pepper, cored, deseeded and cut into strips
For the dressing:
3 tablespoons olive oil
1 tablespoon lemon juice
1 garlic clove, crushed or chopped

Place the endive and tarragon in a mixing bowl. Combine the ingredients for the dressing and pour them over the leaves, tossing well. Arrange the mixed salad leaves in the centre of a serving plate and place small amounts of the endive mixture around the edge, alternating with strips of yellow and red pepper.

Spring greens and peppers
125 g (4 oz) spring greens, finely shredded
2 sticks celery, chopped
2 spring onions, finely sliced
1 red pepper, cored, deseeded and finely sliced
For the dressing:
3 tablespoons sunflower or sesame oil
1 tablespoon lemon juice
1 garlic clove, crushed or chopped
2.5 cm (1 inch) piece of fresh root ginger

Place the spring greens, celery, onions and red pepper in a serving bowl. To make the dressing, combine the oil, lemon juice and garlic in a small bowl. Crush the ginger with the blade of a knife and squeeze it in your hands to extract the juice, letting it drop into the dressing, or you can use a garlic press. Pour the dressing over the salad, toss and serve.

Artichoke coleslaw
125 g (4 oz) Jerusalem artichokes
2 carrots, grated
2 spring onions, finely sliced
For the dressing:
5 tablespoons live goat's or sheep's yoghurt

STAGE II

1 tablespoon lemon juice
pinch of celery seeds
1 tablespoon sunflower seeds

Grate the artichokes. Place them in a bowl and add the grated carrot and onion. Combine the ingredients for the dressing in a small bowl, blending well, and pour over the salad. Toss well and serve immediately.

Marinated kebabs*
1 red pepper, cored and deseeded
12 baby onions or shallots
12 broccoli florets
12 mangetout
2 tablespoons freshly chopped parsley, to garnish
Marinade:
8 tablespoons olive oil
2 tablespoons lemon juice
2 tablespoons freshly chopped mixed herbs
2 cloves garlic, crushed or chopped
1 teaspoon cumin seeds
1 teaspoon freshly squeezed ginger juice

Cut the red pepper into 12 squares, and place with all the other vegetables in a shallow glass or ceramic dish. Combine the ingredients for the marinade. Pour over the vegetables and leave for a few hours or overnight. Thread the vegetables on to 4 long bamboo skewers before serving, sprinkled with finely chopped parsley.

Shredded leek salad
450g (1lb) leeks, washed and trimmed
2 tablespoons live goat's or sheep's yoghurt
1 tablespoon lemon juice
4 tablespoons sesame oil
1 teaspoon black poppy seeds
1 teaspoon yellow mustard seeds

Cut the leeks into fine julienne strips and place in a bowl. Mix the remaining ingredients together and pour over the leeks, stirring gently. Refrigerate for at least 1 hour for all the flavours to combine. Serve chilled.

Courgettes with carrots and nasturtium flowers*
125g (4oz) carrots, grated
125g (4oz) courgettes, grated
25g (1oz) sunflower seeds
25g (1oz) pumpkin seeds
For the dressing:
2 tablespoons walnut oil
1 teaspoon lemon juice
1 teaspoon freshly squeezed ginger juice
To garnish:
nasturtium flowers
fresh basil leaves
Place the carrots and courgettes in a serving bowl with the sunflower and pumpkin seeds. Combine the ingredients for the dressing and add to the bowl. Toss well. Arrange the nasturtium flowers on top and sprinkle over small whole basil leaves.

My favourite salad
mixed leaves of lettuce, endive and lollo rosso
¼ red cabbage, finely shredded
¼ green cabbage, finely shredded
50g (2oz) sprouted alfalfa
1 onion, peeled and finely sliced
1 green pepper, cored, deseeded and sliced
200g (7oz) cooked brown rice
175g (6oz) sweetcorn kernels
2 carrots, grated
125g (4oz) feta cheese, crumbled
1 teaspoon *nori* flakes
a handful of fresh parsley, chopped
75g (3oz) sunflower seeds
75g (3oz) pumpkin seeds
For the dressing:
4 tablespoons olive oil
2 tablespoons lemon juice
2 tablespoons live goat's or sheep's yoghurt
sprigs of rosemary
a few fresh basil leaves

STAGE II

Line a serving bowl with the mixed salad leaves. In a separate mixing bowl combine the shredded red and green cabbage, alfalfa sprouts, onion and green pepper. The easiest way is to turn the ingredients over with clean hands. Fork in the brown rice, then the sweetcorn kernels, carrots and cheese. Spoon this mixture into the bed of leaves. Sprinkle the *nori* flakes, chopped parsley, sunflower seeds and pumpkin seeds on top. To make the dressing place all the ingredients in a screwtop jar and shake to blend. Pour the dressing over the salad. Toss well at the moment of serving to coat the salad well.

*Rice timbale**
225g (8oz) freshly cooked brown rice
1 red pepper, cored, deseeded and chopped
50g (2oz) goat's cheese, diced
1 green pepper, cored, deseeded and finely chopped
3 spring onions, finely chopped
½ small raw beetroot, finely chopped or grated

Place the still warm rice in a mixing bowl and add the goat's cheese. Combine well. Add the remaining ingredients, and mix well together. Spoon the mixture into a lightly wetted circular mould, pressing it down firmly, and refrigerate until cold. Turn out on to a flat plate to serve. The beetroot gives the timbale a wonderful mottled red colouring. Serve with a mixed green salad.

Sweet Things

Seed and Apple Cake
175g (6oz) sunflower seeds
175g (6oz) sesame seeds
150g (5oz) dates, diced
3 sharp-flavoured apples, grated
1 teaspoon ground allspice
apple slices or whole strawberries, to decorate

Grind the sunflower and sesame seeds (a coffee grinder reserved for spices is useful for this). Place in a mixing bowl and add the dates, apples and allspice. Mix well together. Press into an oblong tin and chill well until firm before serving. Decorate with apple slices or strawberries.

Cheesecake*
225 g (8 oz) live goat's or sheep's yoghurt
125 g (4 oz) fresh apricots, stoned and chopped
50 g (2 oz) sesame seeds
50 g (2 oz) sunflower seeds
25 g (1 oz) almonds

Leave the yoghurt to strain through muslin into a bowl overnight. Mix the yoghurt with the apricots. Crush the seeds and almonds and press in an even layer in the base of a cake tin or flan dish. Pour the yoghurt mixture on top and refrigerate for at least 1 hour before serving.

For a real sweet treat, top with Apricot and Vanilla Purée
450 g (1 lb) fresh apricots, stoned and quartered
150 ml (¼ pint) fresh apple juice
150 ml (¼ pint) water
1 vanilla pod

Soak the apricots in the apple juice and water with the vanilla pod for at least 4 hours. Remove the vanilla pod and place the apricots and liquid in a blender or food processor. Work to a purée and serve lightly chilled.

Kiwi and ginger salad
2 kiwi fruits
3 apples
225 g (8 oz) green grapes
1 tablespoon freshly squeezed ginger juice
4 tablespoons fresh apple juice

Peel and slice the kiwi fruit and slice the apples thinly. Place in a serving bowl with the grapes. Stir gently to combine and pour over the ginger juice and apple juice. Serve immediately, accompanied by live goat's or sheep's yoghurt.

Peach Surprise*
4 large peaches
300 ml (½ pint) white grape juice

STAGE II

Peel and slice the peaches and place them in a ceramic or glass dish that holds them snugly. Pour over the grape juice. Leave to stand for 2–3 hours so that the flavour can develop before serving.

9.
STAGE III

Follow this eating plan for days 26–30 of your detox programme.

Keep exactly to the diet plan you have been following in Stage II but:

DAY 26

- Include any steamed vegetables from the following list in ONE meal. They should form only part of one meal; combine them with foods from your Stage II lists.
  asparagus
  beetroot
  broccoli
  cabbage (white, red and green)
  carrot
  cauliflower
  celery
  Chinese leaves
  courgette
  green beans
  leeks
  mangetout
  onions (all types)
  parsnip
  pumpkin
  spring greens
  swede

DAY 27

- Include any steamed vegetables from the following list in TWO meals. They should form only part of each

STAGE III

meal; combine them with foods from your Stage II lists.
artichoke
asparagus
beetroot
broccoli
Brussels sprouts
cabbage (white, red and green)
carrot
cauliflower
celeriac
celery
Chinese leaves
courgette
fennel
green beans
kale
leeks
mangetout
onions (all types)
parsnip
pumpkin
spring greens
swede

DAY 28

- Have up to two meals containing steamed vegetables from the list for day 27. Include any ONE of the following in ONE of those meals (along with any foods from your Stage II lists.)
  Steamed: bass, cod, Dover sole, halibut, hake, lemon sole, mackerel, plaice, turbot, or bean curd (tofu).

DAY 29

- Have a soup or purée made from any of the vegetables in the following list with ONE meal. All other meals today should be of foods from your Stage II lists.

STAGE III

    beet greens
    beetroot
    broccoli
    cabbage (white, red and green)
    carrot
    cauliflower
    celery
    chayote
    courgette
    fennel
    green beans
    leeks
    okra
    onions (all types)
    parsnip
    pumpkin
    swede
    turnip

DAY 30

- Stir-fry any of the foods on this list in olive or any seed oil, and include with ONE meal:
  artichoke
  asparagus
  bean curd (tofu)
  beet greens
  broccoli
  Brussels sprouts
  cabbage (white, red and green)
  carrot
  cauliflower
  celeriac
  celery
  chayote
  chicken
  chicory
  Chinese leaves
  courgette

STAGE III

- daikon
- fennel
- fish
- green beans
- kale
- kohlrabi
- leeks
- mangetout
- okra
- onions (all types)
- parsnip
- peas
- peppers (all colours)
- pumpkin
- spring greens
- swede
- sweetcorn
- turnip

CONGRATULATIONS — You have completed your detox programme, and should be feeling full of vigour and enthusiasm for life (and food!).

RECIPES

Follow the ingredient notes on page 35. All chicken should be free-range or organically reared, and all fish should be fresh, not farmed.

Steamed vegetable medley
225g (8oz) swede
2 carrots, trimmed
1 courgette, trimmed
1 red pepper, cored and deseeded
1 green pepper, cored and deseeded
1 small cabbage, shredded

Roughly chop the swede, carrots, courgette and peppers. Place in a steamer with the shredded cabbage for 3 minutes, or until just tender. Serve with boiled rice.

STAGE III

Japanese-style salad
Select 6–10 different vegetables, some cooked, the majority raw, for example:
25–50g (1–2oz) beansprouts, carrots, cauliflower, courgettes, green beans, mangetout, peppers, radishes, turnips or watercress
25–50g (1–2oz) shredded chicken or prawns (optional)
sesame seeds
sunflower seeds
salad dressings of your choice (see page 37)
Shred, grate and cube the vegetables to provide a variety of textures and shapes. Keeping each type of vegetable separate, arrange in small piles on a large serving dish. Arrange the chicken or prawns, if included, to one side. Spoon two different salad dressings into bowls. Place the seeds in small bowls. Serve immediately.

Juicer soup
If you have a juice extractor, a quick soup can be made from the remainder of any vegetable juices you have used. Once the juice has been extracted from carrot, beetroot, cabbage (and many other vegetables), the remaining flesh and/or peel will be left in a separate container. Simply add this to boiling water, and cook for 3 minutes. Add herbs to taste, and either liquidise or serve straight away.

Smooth soup
3 carrots, trimmed
1 parsnip
1 bunch watercress, well-washed
Chop the carrots and parsnip into small pieces. Place in a saucepan containing enough boiling water to cover and cook for 3 minutes. Add half the watercress. Chop the remaining watercress. Cook the soup for a further 10 minutes. Transfer to a blender or food processor and work to a purée. Return the purée to a clean saucepan. Add the remaining watercress and reheat over a gentle heat. Serve hot.

STAGE III

Mixed vegetable broth
225 g (8 oz) swede
1 parsnip
1 slice pumpkin
2 carrots, trimmed
225 g (8 oz) Brussels sprouts
1 onion, finely chopped

Roughly chop the swede, parsnip and pumpkin, and 1 carrot. Place in a saucepan containing 550 ml (1 pint) boiling water and cook for 5 minutes. Transfer to a blender or food processor and work to a purée. Return to a clean saucepan and add the Brussels sprouts, onion and the remaining carrot, chopped into small pieces. Add a little more water and cook for a further 10 minutes over a moderate heat, until the soup is heated through and the vegetables just tender.

Golden purée
3 carrots, trimmed
1 parsnip
4 tablespoons live goat's or sheep's yoghurt

Chop the carrots and parsnip into small pieces. Place in a saucepan with just enough water to cover them. Cover and boil until the vegetables have almost disintegrated. Liquidise in a blender or mash together. Reheat briefly in a clean pan, and add the yoghurt before serving.

Note: Other good combinations are swede and cabbage or onion and pumpkin. You could purée just one vegetable.

Chicken stir-fry
1 teaspoon olive or seed oil
1 portion chicken, skinned and thinly sliced
1 courgette, trimmed and thinly sliced
1 head broccoli, broken into tiny florets
1 onion, thinly sliced
1–2 tablespoons lemon juice

Heat the oil in a frying pan or wok. Add the chicken and vegetables and cook over high heat, stirring all the time until the chicken is cooked and the vegetables just tender.

Sprinkle the lemon juice over the pan and mix well. Serve immediately.

Chinese-style stir-fry
1 teaspoon oil
1 carrot, finely chopped
1 red pepper, cored, deseeded and finely chopped
1 bunch spring onions, trimmed and finely chopped
6–8 baby corn cobs
1 packet or a large bunch of beansprouts
prawns to taste
Heat the oil in a frying pan or wok. Add the carrot, pepper and onions. Stir-fry briefly and add the baby corn, beansprouts and prawns. Cook for 2 minutes on a high heat, stirring constantly. Serve immediately.

10. NOT JUST FOODS

Simply modifying your food intake is not a fast enough, or effective enough, way to thoroughly cleanse your body. Moreover, your dietary changes alone will only account for one month's work. Radical as this diet is, you have a lifetime's worth of good habits to learn. Simple measures which are neither time-consuming nor complicated will tip the balance for you.

Here are some simple hydrotherapy techniques and other exercises that will help re-energise and de-stress your system. Forming a valuable part of your detox plan, they will also provide the basis for a lifetime's good health. The unique benefits of the detox diet are partly due to its length. You spend one month following the diet, and then return to a much wider eating plan. These exercises can be done every day of your life, whether you are actively detoxing or not. They are all easy to do, yield immediate results, and many of them are lots of fun too.

EPSOM SALTS BATHS

These should be taken twice a week throughout the programme, and can then continue to be a regular part of your own health care. Women should avoid these baths during and immediately prior to menstruating because the effects can be depleting at that time (see addendum.) Do not include these baths in your detox plan if you have eczema, psoriasis or high blood pressure.

Add 450g (1lb) of epsom salts to a hot bath and soak for about 20 minutes, keeping the water hot. Wrap up *well* immediately afterwards and either go to bed or relax completely for at least 2 hours — overnight is best — to allow the process to continue.

Epsom salts are pure magnesium, a mineral required for over 80 per cent of all your body activities on a cellular level. Soaking in its solution allows some magnesium to be absorbed directly through the skin, which makes this a useful tool for combating any muscular aches and pains. It can also provide additional magnesium when the body has most need of it, and has a drawing effect on the skin itself, encouraging perspiration and 'leeching out' impurities. All these benefits aside, it is the most wonderfully relaxing bath, and I often recommend it to people who have trouble getting off to sleep.

DRY SKIN BRUSHING

This is one of the most effective steps you can take to benefit the health of your whole body. It is also one of the most energising and invigorating ways to start the day. You brush when dry, so do it before a bath or shower, using a natural bristle skin brush.

Starting at your feet, brush your skin as vigorously as feels comfortable. Work your way up each leg and up your front and back. Then brush your hands and up your arms. When doing your chest and upper back, focus the brush strokes towards your heart. Finish by brushing down your neck. Do not brush over any skin rash or irritated area.

There are enormous benefits to be had from unclogging your skin by sloughing off the millions of dead cells which fill your pores. By allowing your skin to 'breathe' it can eliminate uric acid and other poisons from your system quickly and effectively, taking some of the strain off your kidneys and liver. The more effective ways you use to eliminate impurities from your body, the better your overall health.

Daily skin brushing also directly stimulates your lymphatic system. One of the lymphatic system's biggest jobs is as your body's rubbish collection service. Running

NOT JUST FOODS

with the blood, it collects refuse from the cells and transports it out of the area and into treatment centres (lymph nodes) where it can be processed and neutralised.

Have you ever noticed that when you get a cold or a sore throat the 'glands' in your neck can become swollen? These swellings are actually local lymph nodes. Large armies of infection fighters will have been mobilised by your body's immune system, and sent to the area under siege. There is a full-scale battle going on there, between your body's own defences and whatever invading organism or local dysfunction is causing the trouble. With all this activity going on, there are inevitably some casualties, and a load of cellular debris. This is all moved to the lymph nodes to be filtered out of your system and rendered inactive. The large influx of material is often more than the node is used to dealing with at any one time, so there is an amount of congestion — seen as swelling.

The largest collection of lymph nodes is in the chest wall, close to your heart, and by brushing in that direction you speed up the rate of flow of your lymph system as well as your overall circulation. More importantly, perhaps, you are ensuring that your lymph system is regularly cleansed, so that there is no build-up of everyday work to slow its response in times of attack.

The most immediate effect of skin brushing on a daily basis will be a much softer skin. Although jumping in the tub or under the shower will still be beneficial, you will not need to use so much soap, and that too will make a difference to the quality of your skin. You will also notice an improvement in any mucus conditions. When the skin starts to open as a route of elimination, the pressure to expel impurities is lifted from the mucus membranes.

COLD WATER PADDLING

This stimulating and refreshing habit will boost your overall circulation and mean an end to cold feet for ever.

After your morning wash routine, fill the bath or a washing-up bowl with enough cold water to cover your ankles. Then paddle. Walk up and down in the cold water for about 2 minutes or 60 steps with each foot. Best of all is an early morning paddle in the sea, so take advantage of it if you have the opportunity. Be careful, though, to pick an unpolluted piece of beach, or you may be doing more harm than good.

This easy cold-water treatment is a boon to your circulation and a boost for the lymphatic system. As your body senses an acute change of temperature in your feet, it radically increases the blood supply to that area in an effort to warm it up. When you step out of the water, your feet feel alive and tingling, and considerably warmer. When you paddle every day, the positive effects are long-lasting, which means goodbye to cold feet in the winter months, and hello to all the benefits an improved circulation can offer.

One patient of mine, a mother of two young children, told me of her first morning's paddling. No sooner was she in the bath, walking up and down, than her children started peering round the door asking what she was up to. 'Paddling', she said, and the cry was up — the children wanted to paddle too, thinking it was a great game. Now they paddle together with her every morning, and when they have friends to stay overnight, it's one of the highlights of their visit!

FRESH AIR

A daily 'dose' of fresh air increases the amount of oxygen available to your cells, improves the condition of your heart and lungs and will exercise your internal organs, as well as ridding your body of excess carbon dioxide.

Many of us work indoors and often the only 'fresh' air we inhale is during a walk to the station or bus stop in the morning, and back again in the evening. This is not quality air — the route often goes along busy, polluted roads, in busy polluted towns and cities.

Trees are the answer. Trees make city air fit to breathe, and account for that 'fresh-air' smell in the countryside.

NOT JUST FOODS

So, if you have a park near you, or a common or a heath, that is the place to take your daily prescription of fresh air. Otherwise, try to plan a walk as early in the day as possible, before the smog has a chance to build up. If this is not possible, what about an early morning air bath? Before you dress completely, throw open a window and take deep breaths while making large circles with your arms. This arm rotation opens up the rib cage and encourages the diaphragm to relax. You don't have to hang out of the window, just stand close enough to it to feel the air on your skin.

The skin shares with the lungs the responsibility for exchanges with the air around us. Your skin breathes too, absorbing oxygen and exhaling carbon dioxide formed in the tissues. Taking deep breaths of air into your lungs while your skin is also bathing in fresh air is an effective way of deepening that connection, and benefiting your whole body.

Every time you take a deep breath your diaphragm relaxes and then contracts, exerting a gentle pressure on your liver, spleen and stomach, and then releasing it. It's rather like an internal massage for your organs.

Striding out and breathing deeply is one of the best all-round exercises available, particularly if you can walk on grass — it exercises the leg muscles more, making for a more effective pumping action, and is less jolting to the spine.

Constipation will not be a worry to you while you are following this programme, but the most effective help for this problem on a long-term basis is walking, taking good long steps and deep breaths, and particularly walking up hills. Think about it — the digestive tract is being squeezed and stretched with each step, which is exactly the effect of peristalsis (the muscular action by which food is moved through the gut naturally). The overall effect is to produce a good muscle tone in the abdominal muscles and throughout the digestive system.

GROANING

This is a marvellous technique for increasing your oxygen intake and de-stressing your entire body. It is totally addictive — once discovered, you will want to do this every day of your life. Like many of the secrets of this programme, it is very simple to do, and profoundly effective. It seems to evaporate stress and tension, and can be a wonderful release for any pent-up energy on an emotional level too.

All you do is lie down — on the floor is simplest, but you can lie on a bed or even a table if there isn't enough floor space. Take a deep breath in, and groan it out. You have to do this two or three times to build up your confidence, and to forget feeling ridiculous, then you will abandon yourself to it. You can groan away any muscle tensions, any bad feelings, any frustration. And, of course, by inhaling deeply you are taking in huge amounts of oxygen.

The effect is amazing. After just a few minutes (and you will find your own natural time to stop) you feel refreshed, relieved and full of energy. I urge you to try this. You can do it in the evening, after a stressful day in the office, at whatever place and time suits you best.

I often use this exercise with the groups that I teach; starting a class in such a dynamic way yields amazing results, not least that people groaning together have overcome any possible embarrassment they might feel at meeting new people. Every person I have shown this technique to is astounded by its effects. Try it!

11. MOST COMMON QUESTIONS

Can I eat potatoes?
Most certainly, yes. Cleaned and grated or shredded they can be included in any of your raw salad meals. I recommend eating only a small amount initially, because the taste and consistency of the raw potato may take a little getting used to.

But what will I drink?
Water, water and water — the most wonderful flush for your whole body. There is the mandatory early morning lemon water, which can be taken again at any point through the day. You may also drink any herbal teas which do not contain orange fruit or extract throughout the day, fresh fruit juices (again without orange fruit or extract), or any fresh vegetable juice (so long as it is not on the restricted list). These juices must be diluted with water to half strength.

Undiluted fruit juices are too acidic for the stomach to deal with comfortably. They will also supply an enormous kick to your blood sugar levels. When you eat a piece of fruit, the natural sugar (fructose) is released into your bloodstream relatively slowly. A glass of undiluted juice provides all that sugar in one instant dose, and is likely to result in a blood sugar low or slump immediately afterwards.

It is sound advice always to dilute juices, whether you

are actively detoxifying or not, and thereby keep your energy levels constant. If you are used to drinking a lot of tea or coffee, this may seem a little daunting, but it really can be easy. In the hot weather there is nothing more refreshing than water or a cool juice drink. If you need a warm drink, lemon water is a wonderful palate cleanser, and tremendously refreshing.

A box of herbal tea bags placed by your kettle makes having a health-enhancing drink every bit as easy as having a toxifying cup of tea or coffee. There are many different herbal tea blends available. In the process of bagging, some of the active properties of the herb have been lost, but care should still be taken not to overdose on any one herb or blend. You should not have more than two or three cups of each tea in a day, but you can mix as many different teas as you like.

Chamomile, peppermint and fennel teas can aid digestion; rosehip and hibiscus or apple and cinnamon are good fruit mixes; lemon verbena and lime blossom are refreshing morning teas. Manufacturers now have trial packs, so you can buy just three or five tea bags, without going to the expense of a whole box. This is a wonderful way to experiment with the different varieties available, without making any costly mistake.

Some herbal teas contain tannin and caffeine — the reasons you have given up regular tea and coffee! Always check the labels and buy only those which state they are tannin- and caffeine-free.

Many restaurants and cafés are only too happy to provide you with a pot of boiled water to which you can add your own herbal tea bag, or you could just ask for lemon tea without the tea!

Almost every bar and pub now stocks mineral water, and it is even available on British Rail and most long route coaches.

Surely I'll get bored?
Have you looked at the recipe sections yet? Have you looked at the pages of foods you can eat? Yes, they are

MOST COMMON QUESTIONS

mainly raw, but your usual diet is probably mainly cooked, and that isn't boring, is it? Nobody ever asks this once they have started the detox programme, and nobody ever looks back at the time spent on it as a boring time. Once you have begun, the tremendous changes in terms of your overall health, energy levels, general vitality, clarity of mind and feelings of 'well-being' will be what fill your mind. Apart from the extra physical and mental energy you will be experiencing throughout the month, you will have extra time, too. It is surprising to realise the amount of time we normally spend thinking about what we are going to eat and worrying about what we have eaten.

The most pressing problem that most of us face when it comes to eating well is that time is so limited. In a world that is moving at an ever-increasing pace, time is at a premium, and fast food is the answer. Raw fruit and vegetables are the ultimate in fast food. What could be quicker than peeling a banana, crunching on an apple, or grabbing a bunch of grapes?

I usually keep a plate of crudités in the fridge when I am working at home. A plate of carrot and celery sticks, some slices of red and green peppers and chunks of cucumber takes only seconds to prepare. With a yoghurt dip, this is a perfect quick snack. Try a handful of mixed sunflower, pumpkin and sesame seeds for a crunchy alternative.

But what if I break it?

There really is little excuse to break this plan. It lasts for one month, and anyone can do anything for just one month. With a little forward planning, you can be sure to avoid any possible pitfalls — you do not have to cancel all social engagements and spend the entire month at home, or miss out on lunchtime get-togethers.

It is just as easy to order a salad as it is to order a sandwich for a lunchtime meal. Most restaurants are only too happy to show their prowess in putting together an exciting mixed salad as a main course, and it might be possible to pack your own lunchbox. If there is not time to prepare lunch in the morning or the night before, maybe there is a greengrocers on the way to work, or a staff restaurant or canteen which can be selectively raided.

All but the staunchest meat-eaters will enjoy a raw meal that is well prepared and nicely presented, so don't miss out on entertaining at home. Dining out at a friend's home need not be a daunting prospect either. The programme you are following is a positive, life-enhancing one, so don't be ashamed of it — most people will be happy to cater to your needs — after all, it's not *that* difficult, and you could always offer to bring one of the courses, or an additional salad.

If you plan for this month, you can make sure that you avoid possible pitfalls — if you are needing to travel, for example, take your own packed lunch or some pieces of fruit, just to be on the safe side. You are making such a wonderful commitment to your body and your health, there will be plenty of time and energy for you to spend a little extra on making sure that your month is a complete success.

What can I expect to happen to my skin?
Skin is one of your largest organs, and along with all your other body systems, it will be stimulated and cleared out through the month. Body brushing will speed up the process, as will the Epsom salts baths, and you will find your skin to be much softer while you maintain these habits.

Expelling toxins through the skin is one of the easiest and quickest routes for the body to take, so you may find occasional spots, which clear up speedily. It is important to allow your skin to breathe well throughout this process, and the one area needing extra attention is the face. Obviously, you will not be using your skin brush there, so cleansing is important. Continued shaving or blocking the pores with make-up can be taxing when the rest of your skin is 'breathing' so freely.

In oriental facial diagnosis (a way of reading the general condition of the body from various parts of the face), the chin is related to the digestive tract, and this is the most common site for any of those spots to appear. Regular gentle cleansing, and giving your face some time to rest — either skipping the occasional shave, or not wearing make-up on some days — will soon leave your face looking radiantly clear.

Why can I not eat regular dairy food?
I think milk, and cheese and yoghurt made from cow's milk, are all great foods — for baby cows. They are no good for humans.

At the chemical level at which digestive enzymes recognise nutrients, size and structure are all important. Think of the size of the average cow, in relation to the average human.

Most cows are much larger and have a much greater body weight than we do. The size of the fat molecules in their milk is also a great deal larger than the size of any fat molecule our enzymes could ever hope to deal with. Sheep and goats, whose body size is closer to our own, have more easily recognisable fat molecules.

When your body can recognise something, it can process it. That is one of the reasons for the great success of this programme — you are building on a centuries-old, established, recognisable way that your body has for coping with stresses.

During the month, you will be eating some goat's or sheep's yoghurt and cheese almost every day. The habit of drinking milk, from whatever source, is something you should have been weaned from at a much earlier age. If you were not, you will be now, through the good efforts of this programme. No milk. Your palate will not want it. Your body does not want it.

Over 50 per cent of the mucus problems that I treat respond to the total elimination of cow's products. That means half the sinus problems, post-nasal drips, chesty coughs and runny noses that people have are either improved or eradicated with this simple dietary step.

MOST COMMON QUESTIONS

Why no animal proteins?
In my experience, some people need to eat meat, others manage better when eating only fish, and some people's health is best when no animal flesh is eaten at all. Determining what suits you is an individual thing, but *everybody*, whatever their preference, habits or needs can manage perfectly well without animal flesh in their diet for one month.

You will not suffer from any protein deficiency during this time. After that, your palate and your food desires will be sufficiently clear to point you in the right direction — your body will be telling you what it needs.

The last few days of the diet allow for a small amount of animal protein to be included. If you are a meat eater or a fish eater (or both) this is the time to reintroduce these foods.

Why start the day with lemon water?
Lemon water is a terrific palate cleanser and therefore a wholly appropriate way to start the day. As the body is left free to continue eliminating and repairing throughout the night, mornings may be marked by a slightly coated tongue and a furry taste in the mouth. This is just a symptom of the impurities being mobilised, and on a programme like this is a good sign. Lemon is also very alkaline, despite being a citrus fruit. Your body generally should be slightly alkaline, and becomes more acidic due to internal and external stresses. Starting your day with lemon water equalises out the work your body has done overnight, and prepares you for the day ahead.

Why can't I eat melon with other fruits?
The first real stage in the digestion of fruits takes place in your mouth. Here, they are chewed into smaller pieces and mixed with an enzyme present in your saliva. Once in the stomach, the fruit is well mixed with your gastric juices and prepared for its passage down through your digestive tract.

Some foods need to remain here for longer than others.

MOST COMMON QUESTIONS

Melon is one of the quickest foods to leave — usually within only 20 minutes of being eaten. It should always be taken on its own to avoid the risk of any other fruits leaving the stomach with it, before they have completed this important step in their digestive process.

Once you have completed the detox programme, and are eating a wider range of foods, melons should still be eaten on their own. Having a slice of melon as the first course of a meal is only advisable if there is to be a delay of more than 20 minutes before the next course.

I have reached the end of the programme, but don't feel like eating much cooked food.
That is fine. Sometimes your body will want you to continue eating a mainly raw diet for a little longer than this month-long programme. During the summer months this will not harm you in any way. It is just a sign that your body is enjoying the diet, and is not yet ready to deal with a more complex food intake.

In the same way as you do not have to force yourself to eat particular foods that you don't have a taste for, if you don't want to eat cooked meals, do not make yourself do so. Once your system has caught up with itself — carried out any healing and repair work that is needed — you will find yourself drawn to a wider range of foods.

12. EXERCISE

Exercising keeps your body in shape in every sense. Feeling yourself move with a mixture of control and abandon does terrific things for your mind, reminding you of childhood playtimes and your body's innate sense of fun. Exercising in a way you enjoy integrates it into your life, and the physical benefits are manifold.

Your body was meant to move. Whether you regard it as a physical carrier for the divine, or 'just' a body, movement is one sure sign of life. Exercise truly does make you feel more alive, and the reason, on a physical level, is simple. Your heart is encouraged to pump more blood. This carries fresh nutrients to all your cells, and, at the same time, your lymphatic system is boosted into carrying away any local debris. Even the smallest blood vessels benefit and your skin will start to glow. As your skeleton changes its position, the muscles that originate and attach to each bone are gently stretched and relaxed. Your energy is diverted from its more vegetative needs (digestion and so on), and towards movement. Your whole body is being used as it was originally designed to be.

You will experience changes on a mental and psychological level too. When your body is pushed to perform physically, your brain produces large amounts of endorphins. These are morphine-like substances, which help with pain relief and also give a natural 'high'. They slightly depress appetite and produce a great feeling of well-being.

Your brain is entirely dependent upon a good supply of freshly oxygenated blood. One quick way to receive this is with a few gulps of fresh air. A long-term way to ensure it is to incorporate regular daily exercise into your lifestyle.

Whatever form or forms of exercise you decide to pursue, you must ensure you wear the right clothing and

EXERCISE

accessories, and get professional advice or training if you need it. Exercise is meant to benefit your health, not cause you any physical problems. In many cases, this just needs you to apply some common sense.

Daily exercise is a fundamental part of your detox plan. You don't have to join a gym, or train for a marathon, but you do need to stimulate your cardiovascular system, get extra oxygen to your cells, and do some mechanical pumping! You need to do 10 minutes each day, more if you want to.

We have talked about walking already, and I cannot say too much in praise of it. It's a way of getting fresh air, a super all-round exercise for your whole body, and it's easy. Almost anyone can fit a walk into their schedule. But the real key to making exercise an acceptable part of your life is to enjoy doing it.

Different people like, and need, different things. For some, the thrill of pushing through their own limits is a tremendous psychological lift. For others, wanting a more sedate form of stimulation, the prospect of a walk in the countryside fits the bill on all counts. So, the first step is to work out what you really like doing. If you like dancing, make sure you make it to a club or disco at least once a week for a good session on the dance floor. If you enjoy exercising with other people then maybe an exercise class is a good idea for you; perhaps this will be the extra push you have needed to get you started in a new sport or activity.

Whatever you *enjoy* doing, that's the way to exercise. If you are spending time in the home, what about doing some of the housework to music? You can 'boogie' with the hoover, and get some extra stretching in that way. If that sounds a little too chaotic, then try running up and down stairs for 5 minutes every day. If you can't positively enjoy your exercise, then at least make it as much fun as possible.

If you have a bicycle, then use it for one shopping trip, or to get to work. The next day you might like to take a brisk walk before dinner. A game of tennis, a short swim or a

EXERCISE

round of golf might be scheduled into your week; or a game of frisbee with friends (or a dog), tree-climbing, running for a bus or a job around the garden. There is currently a craze for having a mini-trampoline in your home; that's great fun if you are looking for something solitary, and so is an exercise bike. And there is always, of course, love-making.

Whatever your choices, the minimum of 10 minutes every day is no great chore, and the benefits are legion. Quite apart from all the possibilities for making new friends and social contacts and the chance of discovering a new hobby, you'll be making friends with your body.

If you are not used to exercising, start slowly. Ten minutes each day should not cause any stresses or strains so long as you don't get too 'gung ho' about it. If you have not done any exercise for a long period of time, then some gentle stretching exercises or a brisk walk are the places to begin.

If you are thinking of jogging or running, get some good, supportive running shoes, and make sure you *never* run on concrete or paving stones. The jolting effect on your knee joints and your spine is phenomenal when you run on such a hard surface. The same advice applies to dance or aerobic exercise classes. Low-impact aerobics are much better than high-impact exercises, and do make sure you are working on a properly sprung floor.

If you are going to use any equipment, as in weight-training or body-building, make sure you are shown exactly how to use it, and how to perform each exercise by a qualified instructor. With this type of work-out in particular, it is essential that you build up your exercise programme very slowly.

If you take sensible precautions, you will be benefiting your body as well as discovering a valuable source of enjoyment. You will be able to find some form of exercise to suit you, whether you are old, unfit, young, healthy or don't have much time to spare. So long as you take a realistic approach, and don't expect too much of yourself initially, the joys of exercise are yours to explore.

EXERCISE

If you want advice on local facilities or general sports information, check in your library, or contact the Sports Council. There is no reason to be stuck for ideas; here are just a few suggestions of sporting activities that you can choose from:

- abseiling
- aerobics
- aikido
- American football
- badminton
- baseball
- basketball
- belly dancing
- body-building
- canoeing
- cricket
- cycling
- dancing
- diving
- endurance training
- fencing
- football
- golf
- gymnastics
- high jumping
- hill walking
- hockey
- hurdling
- ice curling
- ice skating
- javelin throwing
- jogging
- judo
- karate
- kendo
- lacrosse
- lawn tennis
- long jump
- marathon running
- mountain climbing
- netball
- orienteering
- outward bound weekending
- pitch 'n' put
- quoits
- riding
- roller skating
- rugby
- scuba diving
- skiing
- skipping
- sprinting
- squash
- swimming
- table tennis
- trampolining
- underwater snorkelling
- volley ball
- water skiing
- weight training
- wind surfing
- wrestling
- yachting
- yoga

These are mostly organised sporting activities. You can introduce an exercise element into many recreational and leisure pursuits too. Singing is a good exercise for your lungs; it strengthens your diaphragm, and improves the tone of your chest wall and abdominal muscles. Playing a wind instrument does just the same, and 10 minutes of wild drumming is a great arm (and leg) workout, as well as increasing your oxygen intake.

Vigorous leaf collecting or digging can turn gardening into an exercise. At a push, you could incorporate some isotonic exercises into a spell sitting in front of the television!

Finding as many ways as possible to begin exercising means you won't become bored. You'll soon discover the tremendous value of making it a regular event.

13. OPTIONAL EXTRAS

In previous chapters, I have been describing things that are an integral part of your detox plan. There are, however, many other enjoyable ways to support your body in its efforts over this month. Although none of these is essential to the success of your detox, they do provide you with a variety of optional extras to choose from.

Any of these health-enhancing options will support and encourage elimination, as well as providing a natural, healthy treat.

THERAPEUTIC MASSAGE

Massage can be a perfect complement to your detox programme. It will strengthen your resolve to keep up the good work, and greatly uplift your spirits, as well as providing untold physical benefits.

I could wax lyrical about the wonderful feeling of being massaged and the way it seems to integrate physical changes with emotional well-being. On a physical level it improves lymphatic drainage, increases overall circulation, and stimulates your nervous system in a very positive way. It is on another level, though, that its benefits are felt most. Although relaxing, massage will give you the most tremendous energy boost, leaving you with a natural high.

Regular massage serves as a reminder of your changing body shape and image. It will greatly improve communication between your mind and your body as all those nerve endings are gently stimulated, reinforcing your knowledge of your whole body. It is also a great treat. Being able to lie

OPTIONAL EXTRAS

down and let somebody else care for you in a totally relaxed and secure environment is a tremendously enriching experience.

You will find massage therapists at all natural health clinics, and many gyms and health clubs. A full body massage will take anything from 1 hour to 1 hour 45 minutes, depending on the techniques used. You can, though, elect to have just a back massage, or a neck and shoulder massage for example.

You can do some massage for yourself too, on your feet or hands for instance. Get some cream or body lotion and begin by stroking gently, but firmly enough not to tickle. Then increase the pressure and, following the contours of your body, vary the length and direction of your strokes.

You'll soon get an idea of what feels best, and that's all there is to it. If you have a professional massage, you'll pick up some tips for different ways of varying your own massage skill, but your guide will always be what feels good. Sometimes you'll want to stroke quickly, rather than slowly, or press harder in some areas. Just listen to what your body is telling you and you won't go wrong.

There is nothing as effective as a neck and shoulder massage to relieve any stiffness or tension at the end of a busy day. Perhaps you have a partner, or neighbour, or a member of your family who would like to help out here. Exchanging simple massages like this is a wonderful habit to get into. With someone sitting in front of you, you can feel any knots or tight muscles easily through their clothes. Gently lifting or pressing on these areas and 'kneading' the muscles will provide instant relief.

Sensual massage is a rather different experience. Wonderful in its own right for improving communication between lovers and perfect for incorporating into lovemaking, its therapeutic effects are somewhat diminished. Some would say the other benefits more than make up for this.

OPTIONAL EXTRAS

AROMATHERAPY

In massage, cream or gently warmed oil is used to facilitate the work of the therapist's hands. With aromatherapy massage, the focus is different. Oils are always used, to which have been added a few drops of aromatic oil. These essential oils contain many active properties as well as the fragrance of the plants from which they are taken.

In your brain, the area which recognises a smell is very close to a memory association centre. This is why a scent can so often conjure up such clear mental images. A whiff of barley sugar can send me straight into a very secure feeling I knew in my childhood! Absorbing these oils through the skin at the same time as being infused with their particular aroma can be a truly effective mood changer, as well as stimulating a variety of healing activities.

When you consult an aromatherapist, they will select an individual blend of essential oils specifically to enhance or stimulate the way you are feeling and your overall health. There is a host of different oils available, each with its own use.

Jasmine, for example, is a wonderful anti-depressant; rosemary is antiseptic; lavender helps the system overall, and peppermint is refreshing and good for digestive complaints. Eucalyptus and bergamot will often be used for chest congestion and breathing difficulties, clary sage to warm and comfort, and howood for pelvic congestion.

Whether you choose therapeutic massage or aromatherapy massage is up to you. Perhaps following this programme will inspire you to try them both. If you do, you can look forward to hours of relaxed bliss, followed by days of feeling *good*.

STEAM BATHS

Steam or Turkish baths are popular in southern and eastern Europe, and can now be found in most large towns. They are my favourite detox back-up. It always

OPTIONAL EXTRAS

amazes me how quickly they effect the most remarkable clear-out. Within seconds of walking in to a steam room, in fact usually by the time you find your seat, you will feel wet and warm and comfortable. The steam instantly opens all your pores, and perspiration is both intense and immediate. The effect of breathing in all that steam has a wonderful clearing effect on your lungs too.

The best way to benefit from steam baths is to take a warm shower first, then stay in the steam room for about 10 minutes. Then head for a cold shower, and return to the steam. You can repeat this process about three times, but the effects are tiring. It is deeply relaxing and a very thorough skin and lung cleanser, yet at the same time deeply comfortable. The refreshing and stimulating cold showers tone your body and improve the eliminating ability of your skin. If you are just starting to detox or if you have never steamed before, you may need to stay in for a shorter time.

Many steam baths include 'scrub' facilities. At any point you can be washed by an attendant using a fairly stiff brush or loofah which is soaped up to a terrific lather. The lather is to lessen the coarseness of the scrub, which is very invigorating. Very often, this will be followed by a brief massage. The best time to be scrubbed is before your final steam immersion.

Finish off your visit with a cold shower. Once dried and dressed, make sure you rest for a few minutes and have a drink. You can expect to feel very tired afterwards, and quite light-headed. Your body will have worked very hard, and that light-headed feeling is due to the tremendous relief of having shed so many impurities in such a short time.

You will sleep well that night and your skin, already feeling good from your regular skin brushing, will be soft and glowing. Many people also find their breathing is easier, and their chest lighter.

If you have high blood pressure or any heart trouble, care must be taken not to impose too great a strain on your circulatory system. You should check with your practitioner before trying out steam baths or saunas.

OPTIONAL EXTRAS

SAUNAS

Saunas work in a similar way to steam baths by encouraging elimination through your skin, but they use dry heat instead.

The effect of walking into the heat of a sauna is less easy for your body to deal with, but you can remain there for much longer. Saunas often have plunge pools rather than showers, and there is no scrub facility.

They are very common in northern Europe, and in some countries there is one sauna for every four households. Purists would not have a plunge pool, but go and roll in the snow after a sauna, or go for a run in the cold air. The custom of gently beating oneself with birch twigs comes from this part of the world too — the invigorating effects are similar to those of skin brushing, and this is another way to tone the skin and close the pores after a sauna.

If you have poor skin function, or find it hard to sweat, saunas need to be taken for very short periods of time, if at all, to avoid feeling like a pressure cooker. If you have not begun to perspire after about three minutes, leave, take a cold shower or plunge, and try again another day. Do *not* try to sit it out. As you continue your detox programme and your avenues of elimination improve, you will respond to the dry heat more and more easily.

JACUZZIS

Whirlpool spas or jacuzzis are to my mind one of humanity's great inventions. The combination of total immersion in aerated water with deep pressure massage from jets of water is profoundly beneficial.

The French and Swiss have used a variation of this form of water therapy for many years. Called thalassotherapy, high pressure water jets are aimed at the body from a distance, and yield remarkable benefits as far ranging as cellulite reduction and relief of arthritic pain.

Jacuzzis are less specific, but the principle is the same. Sitting up to your neck, or floating in the water, you can position yourself so that the water jets massage either side of your spine, or your feet, or abdomen, or any part of you. The pounding action of the pressurised water reaches deeper than most massage could in comfort. Squashing your muscles up against your skeleton and then releasing them is a remarkable and painfree way of stretching them. It also encourages a mechanical pumping action — essential for a release of any impurities, and an input of fresh nutrients. The total effect is a feeling of tremendous wellbeing.

Ten minutes in a jacuzzi has the same all-round effect as one hour of deep body massage, so care must be taken not to stay in for too long. This is a point to watch, because it can feel so wonderful, you will forget to keep track of the time.

One of my closest friends sent a card from California which outlined a perfect fantasy for me. He was writing it in a jacuzzi up in the mountains one evening. Open to the skies, he was looking up at the moon and surrounded by a fresh snowfall. That image of nature's best and humankind's wonderful inventiveness combined has stayed with me for years. I hope one day to experience it myself.

DOING IT YOURSELF

Many of these treats can be modified for yourself at home. The old-fashioned towel and bowl inhalation is a great chest clearer and a steam bath for your face. Fill a bowl with boiled water and cover your head and shoulders with a towel. Extend the towel over the steaming bowl as you bend down and start to breathe in through your nose and mouth.

Fresh herbs added to the water will enhance the therapeutic effect. Rosemary is a good antiseptic, as is sage. Lemon balm is gently astringent, and rose petals will soothe any sore or inflamed throats and sinuses. Simply rub the herb or flower between your fingers to release any aromatic qualities, and place it in the bowl before adding the water.

OPTIONAL EXTRAS

If you have any sore or aching muscles, a hand shower held under water while you are in the bath will reach right in to any tender spots and speed recovery.

A footbath to which you have added a drop of essential oil or your favourite scent, followed by a foot and then a hand massage will make you feel truly loved and cared for. A drop of lavender oil will soothe away cares and balance your emotions; ylang ylang is used for its sensuous properties; and geranium will lift your spirits.

14.
PUTTING IT INTO PRACTICE

This detox plan contains a lot of new advice — you're going to be revolutionising your eating habits and radically altering your lifestyle for one month. You may be wondering how to accomplish this each day, and make it routine. It is encouraging to realise that once you begin the programme, your renewed physical and emotional energy will quickly give you a tremendous impetus.

Marking the end of your working day and the beginning of recreational time is important. It is too easy, otherwise, to carry any pre-occupations or worries with you until bedtime. One major cause of insomnia is worry about work, or an over-active mind. Making the transition from worktime to relaxation an event in itself will help keep things in perspective.

There are change-over periods in the morning and before bed too. Giving yourself time to wake up properly and assess your feelings before rushing out into the world will keep you on course for the rest of the day. Allowing some time to mellow at the very end of the day will let you relax more easily into sleep.

Having your evening meal before 8 p.m. will leave you with plenty of time to pursue a range of health-giving recreational activities. Too often, eating late in the day can mean there is little energy to do anything other than slump in an easy chair until bedtime.

Once you are into Stage II of the plan, you may well find

your sleeping pattern changes. We all have naturally different cycles. Once your body begins to shed accumulated impurities, you will discover your own rhythm. For some this may mean retiring and rising earlier than before. Others may discover they need much less sleep than usual. Sleeping anything between four and nine hours a night is quite normal, so long as you wake refreshed and are not tired during the day. Each individual pattern may be different, but if it is generated by a healthy body, then it will be what you need.

These patterns are malleable too. Once you know what is best for you, you'll also know what leeway you have. So, if you are a natural lark — needing to sleep well before midnight, and rising early — a few late nights won't hurt, so long as you return regularly to your natural pattern.

I am at my best if I rise early and take a short siesta in the afternoon. In England that is often less than practical, but I try to have an afternoon or early evening nap whenever I can. Many people with Mediterranean or southern European forbears share this tendency, so don't be afraid to experiment and let your body settle into its own pattern. You'll feel much better for it.

YOUR PLAN FOR A DAY

On rising, have a drink of lemon water to cleanse your palate and set you up for the day ahead. Then skin brush, perhaps while running a bath. After your dip, partly refill the bath with cold water for your paddle. You may then like to open the windows for a fresh air bath and some deep breathing while you do some chest-expanding exercises. The few minutes spent on this early morning routine will leave you feeling awake and alert.

Breakfast might be a freshly extracted juice, or a fruit medley topped with yoghurt, or your own selection from the recipe section.

Perhaps you will walk or cycle part of the way to work, or take a short brisk walk at some point during the morning.

PUTTING IT INTO PRACTICE

Lunch might be in a local restaurant or a works canteen, or you may have packed your own. Whichever you choose, remember to make the time to enjoy your meal, taking a proper break. This is especially important for people who work in the home, when it is easiest of all to grab a bite while forging ahead with other things. Working while you eat can interfere with your digestion and is never recommended.

The end of your working day is the time you may well have chosen to pursue a sporting activity, or at least to get your full 10 minutes of exercise. Or you might have decided that this is the best time to practise a relaxation technique, or do the groaning exercise. Perhaps this is one of the days you will have a therapeutic massage, or visit a sauna or steam bath. Any of these will make for a good beginning to a relaxing evening.

An early supper means the rest of the evening is yours. You might choose to have an Epsom salts bath before going to bed, or to give yourself a foot massage. Whatever you choose, make the end of your day as supportive and programme-enhancing as you made the beginning.

Continuing the theme of de-stressing yourself in as many ways as possible, why not plan a totally relaxing weekend? Not everyone can manage to get away to a health farm or spa, but there are many ways to give yourself a pampering at home, and I would strongly recommend doing this over at least one weekend while you are following the programme.

This is obviously easiest if you live alone, but it can be managed with a little forward planning. Perhaps the person or people you live with would like to join you. Maybe, if you have children, they would enjoy spending a weekend with their grandparents. One busy woman I know swapped homes with a single friend for the weekend! Her friend was all too pleased to sample the family life for a few days, and it made a break for everyone.

You will have your own ideas as to what makes for a really relaxing time. Be sure, though, to make it as all-encompassing as is possible. Ideally, every sense should be

PUTTING IT INTO PRACTICE

catered to and given its own special treat.

You can rest your eyes and your mind by not watching television over the weekend. If your job involves paperwork, then avoid any reading at all — get some art books from your library and just look at the pictures! Stock up with some candles, and let them illuminate your evenings. They will rest your eyes and go a long way towards creating a peaceful atmosphere.

If your home is noisy, get some earplugs to enable you to find some silence. Or you might elect to listen only to classical music, and give yourself a cultural fillip at the same time.

Take the telephone off the hook, or leave your answering machine on, so that you will not be interrupted. Taking complete control over your environment for this short time will be wonderfully enriching.

Lighting some incense sticks or burning some essential oils will please your nose and leave your home smelling sweet for days. In the warm weather, putting just a few drops of essential oils in a vase or jug of water will be enough to perfume the whole room. Or add some oils to a small bowl of water placed near a radiator.

Treat your taste buds too. Check your diet plan, and decide what special foods you will have. For me it is always some fresh figs and a couple of mangoes. Do all your shopping the day before if you can, so there is no *need* to go out to the shops if you don't want to.

Sleep when you want to, and enjoy the freedom of not having any constraints on your time. You can do what you feel like doing, when you feel like doing it, and that's a rare state of affairs.

Some massage therapists and aromatherapists will make home visits, so you might like to arrange for one of these, or to go out and have a jacuzzi, or a steam bath. Your sense of touch also needs to be given some time during the weekend, so do make sure that you include some form of tactile nourishment. Nothing makes me feel more pampered than being massaged, so this is something I always try and include whenever I take a weekend break like this.

PUTTING IT INTO PRACTICE

To rest your mind you might decide not to read any newspapers, or have to take in any new information. It might surprise you to find just how hard you work every day in all those little ways. Absorbing the news and keeping track of current affairs and social issues takes a lot of mental energy.

If you are thinking of starting any meditation or stress relaxation exercises, perhaps now is the time.

You can go as far as you want to with this weekend — incorporate as many treats as you like, and do everything to create a very special environment. You can use it to experience more fully your creative talents of painting, writing or whatever, or to simply enjoy doing nothing.

If you work in a town, this would be the perfect time to have some long walks in the fresh air. The complete change of scenery will be a colourful and refreshing break from the often grey uniformity of most towns and cities. We can become indifferent to any lack of beauty in our surroundings, and I think it is important to remember just how easy it is to escape from daily routine and find beautiful places very close to home.

The psychological system of neuro-linguistic programming (NLP) has a wonderful phrase — reframing. Essentially it means to find a new way of looking at an old picture; changing your vantage point or finding a new frame of reference. I never fully understood it until one day when I was waiting at a bus stop on a busy road. I was looking at all the oncoming traffic, studying the buses to try and find the one I needed, and being awfully impatient because I was already running late. The traffic fumes were annoying me, and my stress levels were rising in line with the number of bustling bodies all around me. And then I looked up to the skyline and noticed that the whole road was lined with tall, bushy tress, and the sky was a clear blue, with a few small clouds moving quickly across it. I was struck by how lovely it looked, and how easy it was to ignore the busy street scene all around me while I concentrated on this lovely landscape.

Now, whenever I remember, I try to 'reframe' the sights

PUTTING IT INTO PRACTICE

I see every day. I suppose it is a modern twist on the old saying that 'beauty is in the eye of the beholder'. If you are planning a beautiful, relaxing weekend, though, I think it's certainly worth trying.

There are so many other things you can incorporate into your weekend break. One technique is to close your eyes and imagine the most peaceful idyll you could possibly create, and then set about making it happen.

Don't forget, too, things like Epsom salts baths and other routine body maintenance jobs that you can turn into luxuries. Giving your hair a treatment or doing a pedicure can make you feel as though you are spoiling yourself, particularly if you don't often do them. Women are often better at this than men, but I wish we would all do things like this more often — there really is no monopoly on making yourself feel good.

The emphasis of this programme is on detox, not deprive, so embellish that thought, and plan a luxurious, positive, life-enhancing weekend for yourself.

15. CLEAR YOUR MIND

It would be unfair, at the very least, to follow such a comprehensive detox programme as this for your body, and not spend some time on your mind too.

Your mind and your body are intimately connected, even though we often think of them as being quite separate. Every tiny finger movement you make is controlled by a part of your brain. The way you are sitting now is governed partly by your brain sending messages to your postural muscles, and partly by your state of mind.

If a person is depressed, their body will seem to deflate — shoulders tend to slump, tummies fall over waistbands or belts, even the corners of their mouth will be pointing downwards. If you see someone who is feeling good, though, you'll notice a spring in the step, a head that is held up, and a feeling of expansion about them. These quite dramatic physical differences stem from their state of mind.

Our thought processes and general feelings of well-being send messages throughout the body which govern posture, movement and function. This is the root of the psychosomatic connection, or mind–body link.

There is a lot of mental pollution around. We are bombarded with information and sales talk every time we turn on the television. Walk down any road and you'll see innumerable advertising hoardings and gaudy shop windows.

Silence seems almost impossible to find these days. We are exposed either to constant traffic noise, or low-flying aircraft booming through the skies, or people's car alarms

CLEAR YOUR MIND

bleeping incessantly. Worst of all, to my mind, is the intrusion of other people's radios. In parks or on the beach, they always seem loud enough to annoy, and just too far away to make out exactly what is being played. Shops pipe music through loudspeaker systems, office blocks pipe music into the lifts, and with many telephone systems, if you're put on hold — there it is again.

It could be argued that much of the political and religious doctrine that we are continually exposed to is also a pollutant. We are all certainly exposed to lots of different mental stimuli, and many of these are uninvited.

When your eyes are open, your brain deciphers and records everything in your line of vision, irrespective of your point of focus. Everything you survey is monitored, whether you recognise it consciously or not. That all adds up to a lot of work for your mind to be doing, and an unconscious need for understanding that must be satisfied.

If you are reading a book and come across a word or an idea that is not completely clear, it is well worth stopping to work it out. If you just continue reading, you are soon likely to find your attention is lost, or that your eyes have glazed over. This is because much of your brain is still working to understand that difficult passage. Consciously recognising that, and returning to the spot where you stopped to work it out, solves the difficulty and your full attention can be returned to reading on.

(That sentence is deliberately laboured to illustrate the point. It isn't clear. If you read on now, you may well lose concentration. Go back, and work out that sentence, and your clarity of thought will instantly return.)

This principle is held true by many psychotherapists and psychoanalysts, who maintain that if much of your mind is still trying to decipher early experiences, you won't have the mental resource to respond to new ones.

If we liken the brain to a computer, then we can accept that much more is likely to be going on 'behind the scenes' than is immediately obvious. This analogy allows us to imagine all the steps that make up the chain of our thoughts and actions — if doing one thing elicits a certain

CLEAR YOUR MIND

response, then we set ourselves up to expect that same response each time we do it. We could say that we make our own template, or pattern, and then live by it.

This takes us back to the mind–body link. If you are feeling mentally slumped, your body slumps too. The rolled shoulders and distended tummy so characteristic of this pose are testaments to your state of mind. They will reduce your lung capacity, slow digestive function and weaken muscle tone. Because this psychosomatic link is a two-way connection, your brain is getting reinforcement for its unhappy state from the condition of your body.

While you are following this detox plan, your brain will be receiving many positive messages from your body. There are lots of ways in which you can reinforce these changing signals.

'The power of positive thought' — it sounds a little like a cliché, but affirmations and positive thought repetitions (PTRs) can be powerful agents for change. Making up a motto or ditty and repeating it at times throughout the day is a very effective way to introduce a new mental pattern. And, as we have discussed, your body will always try to prove what you hold to be true — it will try to make it happen. 'Every day, in every way, I am getting better' is a lovely example of an affirmation or positive motto. Repeating your own motto will concentrate your mind upon the idea by repeated exposure to it.

Another richly rewarding way to involve your mind is with visualisations. These actively use your imagination to establish mental pictures — rather like watching a film inside your head. The scenes usually expand to include you as one of the central characters, and with practice, these images can develop into full sensory experiences. You may find the pictures and sensations so strong as to be lifelike, then you will be able not only to see them, but touch and smell, even taste them as well.

Visualisations are like fantasies, or daydreams, only they have a specific purpose. It is advisable to set aside some time especially for doing this, and settle into a comfortable seat. You may choose to picture yourself relaxing on a deserted beach, for example. With the emphasis on relaxation and renewal, you might like to just lie in the sun and feel its rays warming first your skin, then reaching deeper into your bones. Or you might take a walk along the shoreline, have a paddle in the sea, or maybe explore some rock pools.

People sometimes like to make a record of their journeys; you may want to draw some of the scenes you have witnessed, or make a word sketch of them.

This technique has proved effective in stimulating the immune system and helping with illness too. You can imagine armies of infection fighters being mobilised and establishing a defensive cordon around your body. Or small bubbles emanating from your solar plexus and travelling to any area that feels sore or unwell, bringing the energy it needs to feel well again.

Guided imagery is just what it sounds like — the same technique as visualising, but with a director! This person will make suggestions for your changing images, and guide you through different scenarios. There are many tapes on the market which you might enjoy, and they often combine the imagery with relaxation exercises. You can do this for yourself quite easily — all it takes is some practice. Or you could join a class or group. With the aid of a tape recorder you can make revisions to allow yourself more time in certain areas, or to alter the sequence of events whenever you choose.

Leading questions will allow each experience to be somewhat different. Perhaps you might begin with something like this:

Imagine yourself by a waterfall, in a beautiful, lush forest. See the vivid colours, and feel the moisture in the air all around you. Listen to the water cascading down into the pool below, and hear the sounds of the birds and forest animals.

Move a little closer to the pool — What do you see?

Now bend down and cup some of the water in your hands. How does it feel?

CLEAR YOUR MIND

Stay a while and enjoy it.

Turning around, you will see a small clearing where the sunlight pours through. As you move towards it, feel the earth becoming warmer beneath your feet.

What is the view like from here?

I'll leave this for you to finish as you choose. Remember if you make a tape to leave ample time between your spoken ideas for the images to develop and change.

There are many ways to clear your mind. Apart from these more active ways, you may feel drawn to the quieter skills like meditation, or exercises with a meditative element, like T'ai Chi or some forms of yoga.

Meditation is widely used throughout the East, and is rapidly gaining popularity in the rest of the world. There are many schools, each with their own techniques. Despite the difference between particular types, the universal aim is the discovery and maintenance of inner peace and tranquillity. This is achieved in part by the absence of thought. In practice, this means using focusing techniques to still your conscious mind, and stop the endless flow of thoughts that flood through it.

Some people experience this as a quiet time when the freedom from relentless thought patterns allows intuitive images to appear. Others understand it as an inner journey to the depths of their own reality and truth. Whatever your understanding of it, regular meditation can leave you feeling refreshed, alert and centred.

There are different ideas about how often one should meditate. Some say every morning, others feel that starting and ending the day in this way is the most effective. Although making meditation a regular habit is important, and your ability will increase with practice, there are no mandatory rules. Most people agree, though, that real benefits can be gained if you allocate no less than 20 minutes for each session.

Gautama, the Buddha, lived from 563–483 B.C. in India. He is said to have sat in meditation under a lotus tree for many years. This could be where the yoga posture

CLEAR YOUR MIND

called the lotus position originated. This cross-legged way of sitting, with the heels facing upwards towards the heavens, is widely used throughout the Indian continent. In Japan, China and Tibet, a kneeling posture is more common.

The different schools of meditation have many ways of achieving stillness. Encouraging you to focus your attention on another person — usually a guru or teacher — is often used. In Sahaja Yoga, for instance, attention is focused on the guru, Sri Mataji, and this practice is effective whether she is there in person or is represented by a photograph, or even a memory.

Other techniques substitute a sound or mantra as the focus. In Transcendental Meditation, for example, a sound is given to each meditator by their teacher. This sound should be uniquely suited to their needs, and is said to make meditation easier.

Perhaps the most well-known mantra is Ohm. This is repeated, rather like a chant, with the sound changing from the full-bellied Ooo, through to the closed-mouthed Mmm. This can raise your spiritual energy or kundalini up through the body to connect your physical energy with that of the heavens.

One form of meditation used in Zen Buddhism is to pay attention to your breathing — both its pattern and where it stems from. This sounds simple, but it is profoundly effective.

Soto Zen or 'still sitting' means exactly that — finding a still point within yourself from which to observe your thoughts as they pass through your conscious mind. This requires you not to judge them, nor be seduced into following them, but simply to recognise, and allow them to pass on.

Some more modern forms of 'sitting' include using a candle flame or other clear visual stimulus. You look long and hard at the chosen object, then retain the image in your mind as you close your eyes. Focusing on this remaining image concentrates your attention, and frees the subconscious mind.

CLEAR YOUR MIND

Whichever style you choose, and whether you call it sitting, contemplation or formal reflection is a matter of personal choice. A regular practice, though, of sitting still with closed eyes and a clear mind is remarkably rejuvenating.

Yoga is a system of discipline and meditation widely practised within Hinduism. The philosophy is that complete control of the body can free the eternal soul. In practice, this involves a series of exercises, or positions, which develop control over breathing, posture and 'excitation of the senses'.

Valuable as these exercises may be, they form only part of the whole philosophy. Yoga is not something that can be practised for an hour, once a week — it is a way of life. In the East, this is understood. Problems only occur when we in the West try to split off the physical side from the rest of this noble discipline.

I see lots of people who are suffering from back pain as a result of the yoga classes they attend. For some, the gentle stretching exercises can be very useful, but for the many people who are out of condition, or for those who are naturally supple, they can cause problems. It is most important to learn yoga in a small group where you can have lots of individual attention from an experienced teacher. Regular practice is vital too, so even if the class is only once a week, you should practice on your own each day. Finding a good teacher is the key, and they will instruct you on all the dos and don'ts, as well as identifying which exercises you should do, and which to avoid.

T'ai Chi has been described as meditation in action. It is a system of gentle movements which can be performed in a meditative way. There are different styles, notably Yin and Yang (typically, active and passive, or dynamic and containing) and it is taught in different forms. As well as improving balance and co-ordination, it deepens the connections between mind, body and spirit.

This is the chosen exercise of many Buddhist monks and nuns, who find it enhances their mental discipline as well as exercising their bodies. It is very enjoyable to learn, and can be practised just about anywhere. In China, the parks are filled with people doing their own styles of T'ai Chi each morning before work, and during lunchtime breaks.

Resting your mind is important, whether you choose a form of relaxation that exercises your body as well, or one of the more meditative ways. If you do mentally demanding work, have an active imagination or worry a lot, then switching off from all of that will be tremendously rejuvenating. Conversely, if you feel the need to wake your mind up a bit, or increase your mental capacity, then quiet, peaceful reflection will be energising and useful. We all need resting time away from personal and environmental pressures.

You will have done so much to improve communication between your body and your mind while following this detox programme. Don't let the voice of your body get lost in the cacophony of sounds that fills your head. Make a little time each day to declare peace, or at least a period of cease-fire, and let your mind relax. A short detox time every day will clear your mind in the same way that the rest of this programme has cleansed your body.

16.
A WORD FOR WOMEN

Women will experience particular changes while undertaking this detox plan.

It is not a coincidence that the plan takes 30 days to complete — as close as possible to the length of a lunar cycle. Many women will, I hope, take advantage of this, and link the timing of the programme to their own menstrual cycle. This is a plan for spring, so I would recommend beginning with a new moon if possible — a time of new beginnings. A lot of women either menstruate or ovulate with the new and full moons. Some histories tell us that the 'womanly' time to bleed is with the new moon — so that she may see her lover at the time of the full moon; the optimum time to conceive. Other philosophies insist that to bleed with the full moon shows the woman is in possession of her own feminine power.

I have observed that women's cycles change according to the season, their stress levels, and many other life events. Many tend to ovulate with a full moon through the winter months, and have swung round to ovulating with the new moon by the beginning of the summer.

Whatever your cycle, the detox plan will have an impact. Your body is particularly receptive around the time of ovulation. Whether this is at the start of your detox month, or in the middle, the effects will be seen with the following period.

Menstruation is often used by the body as a means of elimination, it is most certainly a symbol of renewal. My experience in this field has shown me time and time again that if there are problems during the month, the period is likely to be heavier or more of a problem than usual. Certainly this is the case if there is food bingeing, if the bowels are congested, if there is any emotional trauma or other health problem. Similarly, if the system is clear, particularly around the time of ovulation, then the period will tend to be lighter or easier.

If there is a history of difficult periods, then there will be a marked change once detoxification has begun. If this is the case and your period is due quite early in the programme, it may well be heavier or lighter than usual, or last longer, or not as long, or cause a little more cramping, or none at all. Every body reacts differently, and whenever there are increased difficulties in the first period, it is an indication of the amount of cleansing needed for the pelvic region. It always leads to a relief of difficulties in subsequent months.

Many women have found that menstruation proceeds very smoothly if they commit themselves to three days on the detox diet each month, at the time of ovulation.

A word here on sanitary protection. At the time of writing, dioxin bleached products are widely available. These may cause a degree of irritation and have been implicated in some studies as being connected with the unpleasant condition, toxic shock syndrome (TSS). A recent American trial showed that women using tampons were likely to bleed for up to two days longer with each period than women using external protection. The suggestion is that this is due to the irritating effect of the tampon on the cervix.

It is for this reason that I recommend not using tampons while on the detox programme, and giving serious consideration to discontinuing their use altogether. Changes are currently being made to bleaching methods, and there are some products on the market which do not contain dioxin. It is not clear, however, whether the prolonged bleeding which has been reported is due to the use of particular products, the absorbent qualities of the tampons themselves, or just the presence in the vagina of an alien object. I recommend patients to suspend use of tampons for a three-month trial period to see how their body reacts.

Women who have had a partial hysterectomy will still ovulate, and therefore continue a monthly cycle, although there is no period. Post-menopausal women, having lived their lives connected to a monthly cycle, still notice their cyclic natures.

You may suffer with the symptoms of vaginal thrush for a few days once you have begun the programme. This is usually mild, easily manageable and by no means a certainty.

The pH scale is a measure of acidity applied to the body. It has a neutral point, and anything above that is considered acid, anything below, alkaline. Your body's pH should be naturally rather alkaline, and many problems caused by dietary and external stresses are directly attributable to the acidity they produce.

The pH of your vagina is inversely proportional to the pH of your body — if your body is alkaline, your vagina will be acid, and this is good. The acid environment makes it an extremely unfriendly place for any unwelcome bacteria or other microbes.

When you change the pH of your body, as you will by following the programme, you will also change your vaginal pH, and thrush symptoms can appear during the change-over. Adding half a cup of cider vinegar to your bath water for a few days is the simplest answer to this transitional problem, and should relieve any irritation, as well as speeding up a return to healthy relief.

Epsom salts baths are not recommended immediately before or during menstruation. Magnesium is a vital ingredient for the abdominal contractions needed to expel the spent lining of the womb. Bathing in, and absorbing, large amounts of this valuable mineral can bring on a period. I sometimes recommend this if there are congestive problems in the pelvis, but do not suggest it under normal circumstances.

Taking these baths while menstruating can prolong bleeding far beyond its healthy range. One patient of mine took one every day of her period, thinking that if one was a good idea, then one a day would be excellent. She came back to see me after bleeding for 10 days, with the expected accompanying low-energy problems. Like any other effective measure, these must be treated with a healthy respect.

APPENDIX — FINDING A PRACTITIONER

The information contained in this book is sufficient for you to undertake the detox programme. If you have any specific health complaints, or feel the need for individual support, or if you want to pursue this natural system of health care, you will need to contact a naturopath.

There are professional associations for naturopaths and dietary counsellors, although not all practitioners join them. Information on the national organisations can be obtained from the Council for Complementary and Alternative Medicine (CCAM), and the Institute for Complimentary Medicine (ICM), both of which are based in London. Most naturopaths do not advertise, but may well be listed in the yellow pages or local equivalent. Some GPs know and work alongside alternative practitioners, so they may be able to recommend one locally.

By far the best way to find a practitioner is through personal recommendation. If someone you know has consulted one and speaks well of them, then this is a good place to start. Always follow your own judgement — it is important to establish a rapport. To feel confident in working with someone, you will need to feel that they are both competent and easy to talk to. You may want to ask them about their training, whether they have any areas of speciality, and whether they have treated people with your complaint before.

Above all, remember that your health and your body are among your greatest assets. It is worth taking time to find the right person, who will be sympathetic to your needs and be able to provide you with professional advice and care.

SUGGESTED FURTHER READING

A–Z of Health Foods, Carol Bowen. Hamlyn, London

The Healer's Art, John Camp. Frederick Muller Ltd, London

Handbook of Herbal Health, Kitty Campion. Macdonald Sphere, London

Knowing Woman, Irene de Claremont Castillejo. Harper & Row

Candida Albicans, Gill Jacobs. Macdonald Optima, London 1990

The Born Again Carnivore, Sue Mellis & Barbara Davidson. Macdonald Optima, London 1990

A Book of Five Rings, Niyamoto Musashi. Allison & Busby, London

Nature's Pharmacy, Christine Stockwell. R.B.G., Kew

Better Health Through Natural Healing, Ross Tatler. Thorsons, Wellingborough

INDEX

acidity, 107
addiction, 27–8
additives, 13
adrenalin, 5, 10, 26
aerobics, 81
agriculture, 14–15
air, fresh, 69–70, 79
alfalfa, sprouted, 23
alkalinity, 107
allergies, 6, 8, 13, 27–8
almond soup, creamed, 46
aluminium, 16, 19
animal proteins, 77
apples: seed and apple cake, 56–7
aromatherapy, 86
arthritis, 27, 28
artichoke coleslaw, 53–4
avocado, 28

back pain, 103
bacteria, in gut, 20, 28–9
bananas, 28
barley, 18
basil: basil and pine nut dressing, 44; basil dressing, 44
baths: Epsom salts, 66–7, 75, 107–8; steam baths, 86–7
bean sprouts, 23
beef, 10
beetroot, 22, 29; summer borscht, 46–7
bicycling, 80
blood circulation, 79, 80
blood sugar levels, 72
body brushing, 67–8, 75
body-building, 81
borscht, summer, 46–7
bowels: bacteria, 20, 28–9; disorders, 6
brain, 79, 97–9
brassicas, 18
breakfast, 92; Stage I, 35–6; Stage II, 41–2

breathing, 69–70, 71, 102
broccoli and ginger, 47
brown rice *see* rice
brushing, dry skin, 31, 67–8, 75
BSE, 10
Buddha, 101–2

cabbage: cabbage, thyme and feta crumble, 48; red and white coleslaw, 47–8; sesame cabbage, 48
caffeine, 26, 31, 73
cake, seed and apple, 56–7
calcium, 28
candida, 29
candle gazing, 102
canned foods, 19
carbohydrates, 10
cardiovascular system, 79, 80
carrots: carrot and daikon, 48–9; carrot with garlic, ginger and cumin, 49; courgettes with carrots and nasturtium flowers, 55; golden purée, 64
cauliflower coated with cheese, 49
cayenne, 21
celery: celery and goat's cheese wheels, 51; celery bundles, 50; celery sticks filled with feta, 49–50
cellulite, 3
cellulose, 20
cereals, 18, 27
chayote with basil and pumpkin seeds, 51
cheese, 44, 76; cabbage, thyme and feta crumble, 48; cauliflower coated with cheese, 49; celery and goat's cheese wheels, 51; celery sticks filled with feta, 49–50; courgette and leeks with feta and yoghurt, 51–2; cucumber cups, 52

INDEX

cheesecake, 57
chicken stir-fry, 64–5
chicory and fennel in coriander dressing, 50–1
China, 11
Chinese-style stir-fry, 65
chlorophyll, 23
chocolate, 31
cholesterol, 23, 26
circulatory problems, 69
coated tongues, 31, 77
coconut, 28
coffee, 2, 5, 26, 31, 73
cold summer soup, 46
cold water paddling, 31, 68–9
colds, 21, 31, 68
coleslaw: artichoke coleslaw, 53–4; red and white coleslaw, 47–8
constipation, 6, 70
cooked food, 78
coriander dressing, 45, 50–1
corn, 18
Council for Complementary and Alternative Medicine (CCAM), 109
courgettes: courgette and leeks with feta and yoghurt, 51–2; courgette dressing, 45; courgettes with carrots and nasturtium flowers, 55
cravings, 31
creamed almond soup, 46
crudités, 74
cucumber: cold summer soup, 46; cucumber cups, 52
cycling, 80

daikon, carrot and, 48–9
dairy products, 76
dancing, 80, 81
daydreams, 99–101
degenerative diseases, 6
depression, 97
diarrhoea, 6
dietary counsellors, 109
dinner: Stage I, 36–7; Stage II, 42–4
dressings, 44–5
dried fruit salad, 39
drinks, 15–17, 72–3

dry skin brushing, 31, 67–8, 75
dyspepsia, 6

eczema, 66
Egypt, Ancient, 11
emotions, 32
endive: endive boats, 52; endive with tarragon, 52–3
endorphins, 79
entertaining, 74–5
Epsom salts baths, 66–7, 75, 107–8
essential oils, 86, 90, 94
European Commission, 16
exercise, 31, 70, 79–83, 93
eyes, resting, 94

face, steaming, 89
facial diagnosis, 75–6
fantasies, 99–101
farming, 14–15
fats, 10, 28
favourite breakfast juice, 39
favourite salad, 55–6
feet: cold water paddling, 31, 68–9; footbaths, 90
fennel: chicory and fennel in coriander dressing, 50–1; fennel dressing, 45
'fight or flight' response, 5–6, 26
filters, water, 17
fish, 15, 77
flour, 19, 27
fluoride, 16
footbaths, 90
fresh air, 69–70, 79
fructose, 72
fruit, 74; digestion, 77–8; 'no' foods, 28; peeling, 44; juices, 24–5, 39–40, 72–3; Stage I, 35; Stage II, 41–2
fruit salads: dried fruit salad, 39; kiwi and ginger salad, 57
Fu Hsi, Emperor, 11
fungi, 29

gallstones, 6
gardening, 83
garlic, 21–2, 24; carrot with garlic, ginger and cumin, 49;

INDEX

cauliflower coated with cheese, 49
ginger, 21; broccoli and ginger, 47; carrot with garlic, ginger and cumin, 49; kiwi and ginger salad, 57
goat's cheese, 76
golden purée, 64
green yoghurt dressing, 45
groaning, 71
guided imagery, 100–1

headaches, 31
healing crisis, 31, 32
heart, exercise, 79, 80
herbal teas, 72, 73
herbalism, 11–12
herbs, steam inhalation, 89
high blood pressure, 66
Hinduism, 11, 103
hydrotherapy, 66–7, 68–9
hysterectomy, 107

imagery, guided, 100–1
immune system, 32, 68, 100
India, 11
inhaling steam, 89
insomnia, 91
Institute for Complimentary Medicine (ICM), 109
iodine, 21
isotonic exercises, 83

jacuzzis, 88–9
Japanese-style salad, 63
Jerusalem artichokes: artichoke coleslaw, 53–4
jogging, 81
juicer soup, 63
juices, 24–5, 39–40, 72–3

kebabs, marinated, 54
kelp, 21
kiwi and ginger salad, 57

lead pollution, 16
leeks: courgette and leeks with feta and yoghurt, 51–2; shredded leek salad, 54–5
lemon water, 37, 72, 73, 77

lentils, 28
live muesli, 38–9
liver, 6, 22
love-making, 81, 85
low water cooking, 38
lunch, 93; Stage I, 36–7; Stage II, 42–4
lymphatic system, 67–8, 79, 84

magnesium, 67, 107–8
mantras, 102
marinated kebabs, 54
massage: aromatherapy, 86; feet and hands, 90; jacuzzis, 88–9; therapeutic massage, 84–5
Mataji, Sri, 102
meat, 10, 14–15, 77
medicines, foods as, 11–12
meditation, 101–3
melon, 77–8
menstruation, 66, 105–8
metabolism, 7
migraine, 28
milk, 7, 76
mind, clearing, 97–104
mineral water, 17, 73
minerals, 10, 12, 19, 33–4
mixed vegetable broth, 64
muesli, live, 38–9
multi-vitamin supplements, 33–4
muscles, sore and aching, 90
mushrooms, 29
my favourite breakfast juice, 39
my favourite salad, 55–6

nasturtium flowers, courgettes with carrots and, 55
naturopathy, 2, 109
neuro-linguistic programming (NLP), 95
noise, 97–8
nori, 21

oils: cooking, 44; essential, 86, 90, 94
oranges, 29
organic foods, 12–15
ovulation, 105, 106
oxalic acid, 28
oxygen, 69–70, 71, 79, 80

113

INDEX

paddling, cold water, 31, 68–9
parsley, 22
peach surprise, 57–8
peanuts, 28
peppers, spring greens and, 53
periods, 105–8
pesticides, 7, 16
pH scale, 107
piles, 6
pine nuts: basil and pine nut dressing, 45
pollution, mental, 97–8
positive thought repetitions (PTRs), 99
potatoes, 72
proteins, 10, 77
psoriasis, 66
psychosomatic connection, 97, 99
pumpkin seeds, chayote with basil and, 51
purée, golden, 64

raw food, 74, 78
reading, 94, 98
recipes: Stage I, 37–40; Stage II, 44–58; Stage III, 62–5
red and white coleslaw, 47–8
reframing, 95–6
relaxation, 91–2, 93–6, 104
religions, dietary rules, 11–12
restaurants, 74–5
rhubarb, 28
rice, 18, 19–20; boiled brown rice, 37–8; rice timbale, 56
running, 81

Sahaja Yoga, 102
salads, 36–7; 47–56, 74; artichoke coleslaw, 53–4; broccoli and ginger, 47; cabbage, thyme and feta crumble, 48; carrot and daikon, 48–9; carrot with garlic, ginger and cumin, 49; celery and goat's cheese wheels, 51; celery bundles, 50; celery sticks filled with feta, 49–50; chayote with basil and pumpkin seeds, 51; chicory and fennel in coriander dressing, 50–1; courgette and leeks with feta and yoghurt, 51–2; courgettes with carrots and nasturtium flowers, 55; cucumber cups, 52; endive boats, 52; endive with tarragon, 52–3; Japanese-style salad, 63; marinated kebabs, 54; my favourite salad, 55–6; red and white coleslaw, 47–8; rice timbale, 56; sesame cabbage, 48; shredded leek salad, 54–5; spring greens and peppers, 53
saliva, 77
Sandra's special (juice), 40
sanitary protection, 106–7
saunas, 88
sea vegetables, 20–1
seed and apple cake, 56–7
sensual massage, 85
sesame cabbage, 48
sheep's cheese, 76
shredded leek salad, 54–5
silence, 97–8
singing, 82–3
sinus conditions, 31
skin, 75–6; breathing, 70; dry skin brushing, 31, 67–8; 75; problems, 31; saunas, 88; steam baths, 87
sleep, 91–2
smooth soup, 63
sorrel, 28
Soto Zen, 102
soups, 46–7; cold summer soup, 46; creamed almond soup, 46; juicer soup, 63; mixed vegetable broth, 64; smooth soup, 63; summer borscht, 46–7
spices, 21
spinach, 28
sports, 82
spots, 75–6
spring greens and peppers, 53
sprouts, 23
steam baths, 86–7
steam inhalation, 89
steamed vegetable medley, 59
stimulants, 26

INDEX

stress, 1, 5–7
stretching exercises, 103
sugar, 5
summer borscht, 46–7
summer juice treat, 40
sweet recipes, 56–8

T'ai Chi, 101, 103–4
tampons, 106–7
tannin, 73
taste buds, 16
tea, 16–17, 26, 31, 73
teas, herbal, 72, 73
thalassotherapy, 88
thirst quencher, 40
thrush, 107
timbale, rice, 56
tomatoes, 28
tongue, coated, 31, 77
toxic shock syndrome (TSS), 106
Transcendental Meditation, 102
trees, 69–70
tropical juice, 40
Turkish baths, 86–7

ulcers, 6
uric acid, 67
urine, 22, 34

vaginal thrush, 107
vegetables, 8, 74; juices, 24–5, 72–3; low water cooking, 38; 'no' foods, 28; peeling, 44; sea vegetables, 21; Stage I, 36–7; Stage II, 43–4; Stage III, 59–62; steamed vegetable medley, 59; see also salads, soups and individual types of vegetable
visualisations, 99–101
vitamins, 10, 12, 19, 23, 33–4
vitamin B complex, 19, 27, 34
vitamin B12, 23
vitamin C, 19, 21, 29, 33–4

wakame, 21
walking, 69–70, 80
water: cold water paddling, 31, 68–9; drinking, 15–17, 72–3; jacuzzis, 88–9
weekends, 93–6
weight fluctuations, 6, 32
weight-training, 81
wheat, 18, 27
whirlpool spas, 88–9
women, menstruation, 105–8

yoga, 101, 103
yoghurt, 44, 76; cheesecake, 57; courgette and leeks with feta and yoghurt, 51–2; green yoghurt dressing, 45; yoghurt crumble, 45; yoghurt dressing, 45

Zen Buddhism, 102

MORE BOOKS FROM OPTIMA

Immune Power by Jennifer Meek

The immune system has an amazing capacity to fight illness and disease, but its inefficiency or breakdown can have serious consequences for our health and is related to a variety of conditions, from lacking energy to ME, from recurrent colds to cancer.

This guide shows how you can strengthen and enhance your immune system and with a positive attitude enjoy a healthy, active and long life. Written by a qualified nutritional counsellor, it identifies particular diseases and illnesses and covers topics such as diet and nutrition, vitamins and minerals, exercise and sleep, stress and depression, and the environment and pollution.

Price (in UK only) £5.99
ISBN 0 356 17138 8

A Matter of Life by Dr. Nadya Coates and Norman Jollyman

The Springhill Centre is a rehabilitation, respite and terminal care centre with a revolutionary approach to the treatment of degenerative and disabling illnesses, including cancer, leukaemia, AIDS, cerebral palsy, spina bifida, multiple sclerosis and strokes.

Emphasising the responsibility of patients for their own health and quality of life, *A Matter of Life* presents the self-help philosophy of Springhill as it outlines ways of improving your health through diet and nutrition, exercise, detoxification, pain control, stress management, relaxation and visualisation. Integrating orthodox medical treatments with a variety of complementary therapies, its affirmative approach offers renewed aspirations, wider horizons and new possibilities for healthcare for people with serious or life-threatening illnesses.

Price (in UK only) £6.99
ISBN 0 356 19107 9

Candida Albicans by Gill Jacobs

What is Candida albicans? How is it linked to ME, digestive disorders, cystitis, depression, menstrual problems, multiple sclerosis? What can be done to help?

Candida Albicans presents a probing and objective account of how health problems may develop when the balance of the candida yeast fungus inside all our bodies is disturbed — often by extensive use of antibiotics, steroids or the pill, by an unhealthy diet and stress, or by inherited problems with immunity. On the basis of extensive interviews, Gill Jacobs evaluates the attitudes and experiences of patients, some of whom were ill for many years before gaining recognition, as well as examining the varied approaches to treatment.

Price (in UK only) £5.99
ISBN 0 356 18685 7

Encyclopaedia of Natural Medicine by Michael Murray and Joseph Pizzorno

The *Encyclopaedia of Natural Medicine* is the most comprehensive guide and reference to the use of natural measures in the maintenance of good health and the prevention and treatment of disease. It explains the principles of natural medicine and outlines their application through the safe and effective use of herbs, vitamins, minerals, diet and nutritional supplements, and covers an extensive range of health conditions, from asthma to depression, from psoriasis to candidiasis, from diabetes to the common cold.

Drawing on the centuries-old wisdom of the healing powers of nature, and supported with modern scientific investigation, the *Encyclopaedia* is the ultimate guide to a natural, healthy lifestyle.

Michael Murray is a leading researcher in the field of natural medicine and a member of the faculty of Bastyr College, one of the world's foremost naturopathic colleges. Joseph Pizzorno is a prominent educator in natural medicine, and the President and co-founder of Bastyr College.

Price (in UK only) £12.99
ISBN 0 356 17218 X

All Optima books are available at your bookshop or newsagent, or can be ordered from the following address:

Optima, Cash Sales Department,
PO Box 11, Falmouth, Cornwall TR10 9EN

Please send cheque or postal order (no currency), and allow 60p for postage and packing for the first book, plus 25p for the second book and 15p for each additional book ordered up to a maximum charge of £1.90 in the UK.

Customers in Eire and BFPO please allow 60p for the first book, 25p for the second book plus 15p per copy for the next 7 books, thereafter 9p per book.

Overseas customers please allow £1.25 for postage and packing for the first book and 28p per copy for each additional book.